Lecture Notes in Computer Science 16499

Founding Editors

Gerhard Goos
Juris Hartmanis

Editorial Board Members

Elisa Bertino, *Purdue University, West Lafayette, IN, USA*
Wen Gao, *Peking University, Beijing, China*
Bernhard Steffen, *TU Dortmund University, Dortmund, Germany*
Moti Yung, *Columbia University, New York, NY, USA*

The series Lecture Notes in Computer Science (LNCS), including its subseries Lecture Notes in Artificial Intelligence (LNAI) and Lecture Notes in Bioinformatics (LNBI), has established itself as a medium for the publication of new developments in computer science and information technology research, teaching, and education.

LNCS enjoys close cooperation with the computer science R & D community, the series counts many renowned academics among its volume editors and paper authors, and collaborates with prestigious societies. Its mission is to serve this international community by providing an invaluable service, mainly focused on the publication of conference and workshop proceedings and postproceedings. LNCS commenced publication in 1973.

Clément Pit-Claudel · Katherine Kosaian
Editors

Verified Software

Theories, Tools and Experiments

17th International Conference, VSTTE 2025
Menlo Park, CA, USA, October 6, 2025
Revised Selected Papers

 Springer

Editors
Clément Pit-Claudel
EPFL
Lausanne, Switzerland

Katherine Kosaian
University of Iowa
Iowa City, IA, USA

ISSN 0302-9743   ISSN 1611-3349 (electronic)
Lecture Notes in Computer Science
ISBN 978-3-032-27339-0   ISBN 978-3-032-27340-6 (eBook)
https://doi.org/10.1007/978-3-032-27340-6

Preface

This volume contains the papers presented at VSTTE 2025: the 17th International Conference on Verified Software: Theories, Tools, and Experiments, held on October 6, 2025 in Menlo Park, California. It was co-located with Formal Methods in Computer-Aided Design 2025.

The program included 6 papers (4 regular long papers and 2 short papers) and 2 work-in-progress presentations chosen out of 17 submissions (9 regular long papers, 6 regular short papers, and 2 work-in-progress) using single-blind reviews. Two submissions were desk rejected, both of which were regular short papers. Work-in-progress papers were accepted for presentation only. Some selected papers that were not accepted to the post-proceedings were invited to present under the work-in-progress track instead. Each submission, except for the two that were desk rejected, was reviewed by 3 program committee members. The paper "Template DBM: A New Weakly Relational Domain for Efficient Memory-Access Validation" by Yusen Su, Jorge Navas, and Arie Gurfinkel was selected for the Best Tool Paper Award. The program also included two invited talks and one long-form invited tutorial. Caroline Trippel (Stanford University) gave an invited talk titled "Design and Formal Verification of Hardware-Software Security Contracts" and Grant Passmore (Imandra) gave an invited talk titled "Formal Verification of Financial Infrastructure with Imandra". Pierre-Yves Strub (PQShield) gave a tutorial on EasyCrypt. The proceedings additionally include extended abstracts by Caroline Trippel and Pierre-Yves Strub, which were individually reviewed by the PC chairs prior to inclusion.

The goal of the VSTTE conference series is to advance the state of the art in the science and technology of software verification, through the interaction of theory development, tool evolution, and experimental validation. The Verified Software Initiative (VSI), spearheaded by Tony Hoare and Jayadev Misra, is a research program for making large-scale verified software a practical reality. The International Conference on Verified Software: Theories, Tools, and Experiments (VSTTE) is the main forum for advancing the initiative. VSTTE brings together experts spanning the spectrum of software verification in order to foster international collaboration on critical research challenges. The theoretical work includes semantic foundations and logics for specification and verification, and verification algorithms and methodologies. The tools cover specification and annotation languages, program analyzers, model checkers, interactive verifiers and proof checkers, automated theorem provers and SAT/SMT solvers, and integrated verification environments. The experimental work drives the research agenda for theory and tools by taking on significant specification/verification exercises covering hardware, operating systems, compilers, computer security, parallel computing, and cyber-physical systems.

November 2025

Katherine Kosaian
Clément Pit-Claudel

Organization

Program Committee Chairs

Katherine Kosaian   University of Iowa, USA
Clément Pit-Claudel   EPFL, Switzerland

Steering Committee

Supratik Chakraborty   IIT Bombay, India
Natarajan Shankar   SRI International, USA

Program Committee

Mario Carneiro   Chalmers University of Technology, Sweden
Julien Deantoni   Université Côte d'Azur, France
Peter Höfner   Australian National University, Australia
Geoff Hulette   Amazon Web Services, USA
Inigo Incer   University of Michigan, USA
Shachar Itzhaky   Technion, Israel
Bettina Könighofer   Graz University of Technology, Austria
Nikolai Kosmatov   Thales Research & Technology, France
Patrick Lam   University of Waterloo, Canada
Jianwen Li   East China Normal University, China
Ruben Martins   Carnegie Mellon University, USA
Nina Narodytska   VMware Research by Broadcom, USA
Andrei Paskevich   Université Paris-Saclay, France
Aseem Rastogi   Microsoft, India
Philipp Rümmer   University of Regensburg, Germany
Natasha Sharygina   Università della Svizzera Italiana, Switzerland
Oleg Sokolsky   University of Pennsylvania, USA
Cynthia Sturton   University of North Carolina at Chapel Hill, USA
Laura Titolo   Code Metal, USA
Beta Ziliani   Universidad ORT Uruguay, Uruguay

Additional Reviewers

Grigory Fedyukovich

Tomáš Kolárik

Jean-Christophe Filliâtre

Marco A. Feliu

Frédéric Recoules

Stefan Pranger

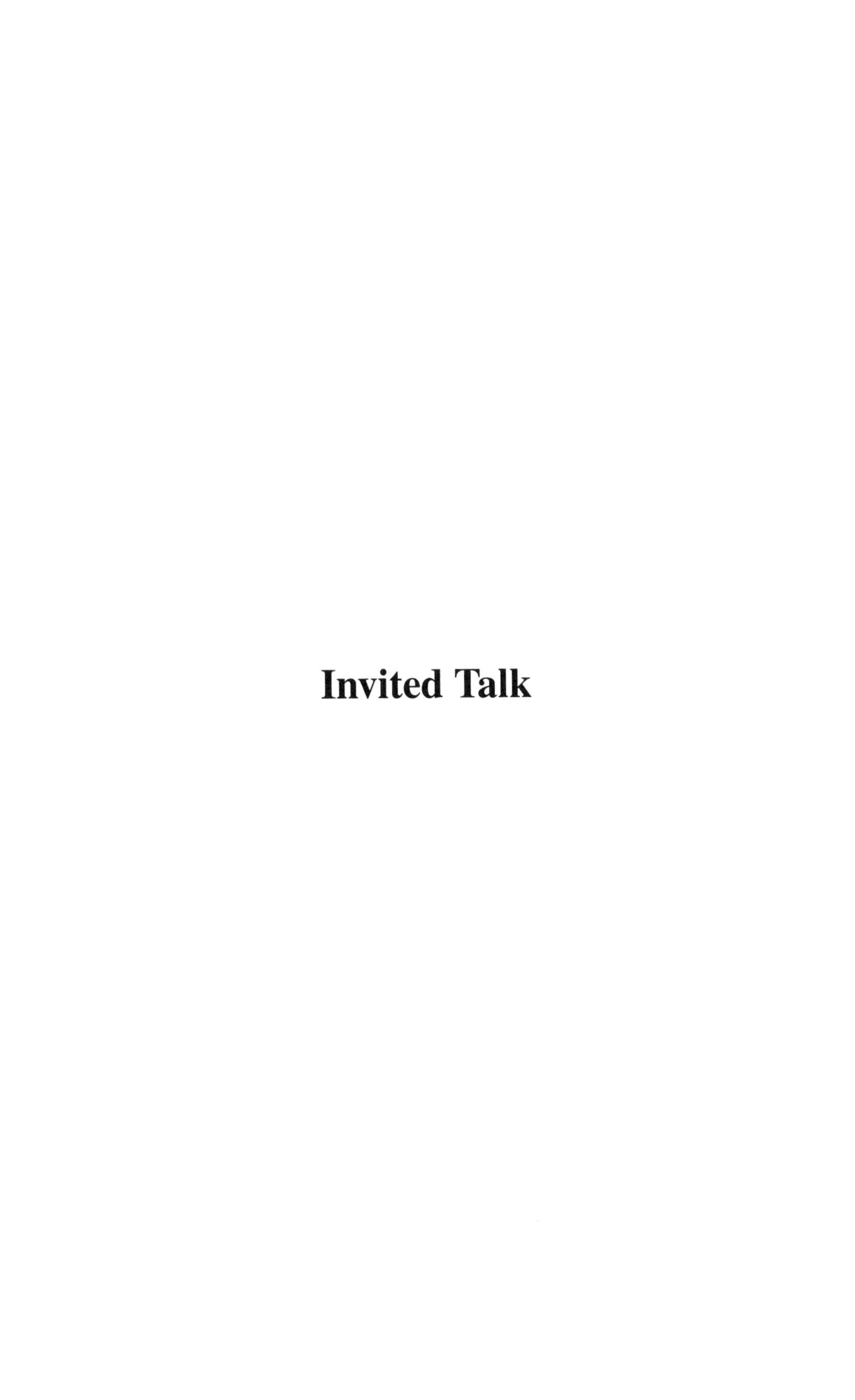

Invited Talk

Design and Formal Verification of Hardware-Software Security Contracts

Caroline Trippel

Computer Science and Electrical Engineering Departments, Stanford University,
Stanford CA, 94305
`trippel@stanford.edu`

Hardware side-channel attacks occur when a victim program's hardware resource usage is influenced by a secret, and an attacker observes this resource usage (e.g., via its effect on execution time) to infer the secret's value. Hardware side-channel attacks were once thought to threaten only secret-processing code and to be mitigated by *constant-time programming*, which avoids passing secrets to the unsafe operands of *transmitter* instructions,[1] which leak said operands via hardware side channels. However, Spectre attacks reveal that transient execution of instructions along mispredicted code paths can leak victim secrets, even if they are never leaked (via transmitters) or even accessed architecturally. These attacks bypass gold standard software-level security policies (e.g., constant-time programming and sandboxing), establishing hardware side-channel attacks as a threat to all programs that hold secrets in architectural state.

All hardware side-channel defenses, including Spectre defenses, require cooperation between hardware and software. We decompose this cooperation into five components: a leakage contract, an execution contract, a protection set, a protection mechanism, and a secret set. A leakage contract characterizes a microarchitecture's transmitters, while an execution contract characterizes its control- and data-flow semantics, possibly taking into account transient execution (e.g., caused by hardware mispredictions). Together, they characterize the vulnerability of a baseline microarchitecture (hardware implementation) to hardware side-channel attacks. A protection set defines the set of architectural states at each program point that a hardware side-channel defense promises to prevent from leaking, while a protection mechanism defines how the defense enforces its protection set (prevents its contents from leaking) and under what circumstances (architecturally and/or transiently). Together, they define a hardware side-channel defense that extends a baseline microarchitecture. Finally, a secret set defines the set of all architectural states at each program point that may hold secret program data, while ensuring that the defense's protection set always contains all secrets. In other words, this component defines the class of vulnerable programs that the defense can secure.

State-of-the-art hardware side-channel defenses minimally require hardware to implement its leakage contract and execution contract components correctly. Compared to execution contracts, leakage contracts are relatively mature. Several leakage contracts

---

[1] Vladimir Kiriansky et al. "DAWG: A Defense Against Cache Timing Attacks in Speculative Execution Processors". In: *51st Annual IEEE/ACM International Symposium on Microarchitecture (MICRO)*. 2018.

have emerged in academic literature and industry documentation to support a variety of performant hardware side-channel defenses. However, an automated approach for formally verifying hardware adherence to a given leakage contract remains elusive. Execution contracts, on the other hand, are less well-established. In particular, it is unclear how best to restrict microarchitectural control- and data-flow so that defenses against Spectre attacks are both feasible and performant.

In this talk, I presented our work on addressing both challenges above. First, I introduced our work on designing a novel execution contract, called ASP, which enables efficient defenses against Spectre attacks in software, and a corresponding compiler defense, called Serberus, for hardening constant-time code (e.g., cryptographic code) against Spectre on hardware that upholds ASP. Second, I discussed an automated approach and tool we designed, called SynthLC, for formally verifying that a given SystemVerilog processor design correctly implements the leakage contracts it claims to.

1 Serberus: A Hardware Execution Contract-Enabled Software Spectre Defense

Serberus is the first defense to secure constant-time programs against Spectre attacks involving any combination of the following five pervasive types of speculation on existing hardware: conditional branch prediction (PHT), indirect branch prediction (BTB), return address prediction (RSB), store-to-load forwarding (STL), and predictive store forwarding (PSF).[2] Serberus assumes that hardware implements the established constant-time leakage contract, which consists of a list of (transmitter, unsafe-operand) pairs, and a novel execution that contract we developed, called ASP. Serberus' protection set consists of the (implicit/explicit) outputs of a special class of instructions we identify, called taint-primitives, and it mixes new and old protection mechanisms, namely code rewriting at compile time and speculation fence insertion. Serberus is designed to secure a slightly restricted class of constant-time programs, which I referred to as CTS* programs in this talk. We arrived at this design for Serberus by overcoming several fundamental challenges facing compile-time Spectre defenses, two of which I discussed in detail: making transient control-flow analysis tractable and root-causing Spectre leakage of secrets in constant-time code.

1.1 Making Transient Control-Flow Analysis Tractable

By default, hardware exhibits unconstrained transient control-flow, which is intractable to reason about in software. For example, return instructions can transiently return to any instruction in the program, including ones hidden within compiled instructions (e.g., due to variable-length instruction encodings). Further, calls can transiently jump to any instruction, including hidden ones. The result is a messy transient control-flow graph that is impossible to analyze at compile time.

---

[2] Nicholas Mosier et al. "Serberus: Protecting cryptographic code from spectres at compile-time". In: *45th IEEE Symposium on Security and Privacy (SP)*. 2024.

Our solution is to constrain transient control-flow using existing control-flow integrity (CFI) instruction set architecture (ISA) extensions, such as Intel Control-Flow Enforcement Technology (CET) for Serberus. Intel originally proposed the architectural semantics of CET in 2016; however, we found that if its transient semantics were to mirror its architectural semantics, we could use it to judiciously constrain a program's transient control-flow at compile time to the point that it could be reasoned about by software analyses. Through discussions with our Intel collaborators, we confirmed that CET's transient semantics mirror its architectural semantics on Intel efficiency-core microarchitectures with the help of the "RRSBA disable" speculation control, which prevents return address predictions from being serviced by the indirect branch predictor.

Thus, Serberus leverages Intel CET as follows. First, it enables CET's indirect branch tracking feature, which ensures that calls and jumps only transiently jump to ENDBRANCH instructions, which Seberus inserts at each function entrypoint. Next, Serberus enables CET's shadow stack and the "RRSBA disable" speculation control, which together ensure returns can only return to callsites. Notably, CET alone is not a Spectre defense. However, on the aforementioned microarchitectures it sufficiently restricts the transient control-flow paths along which a program's secret data may leak. The ASP execution contract that Serberus assumes, which we define as an operational model, captures these transient control-flow restrictions.

1.2 Root-Causing Spectre Leakage in Constant-Time Code

To reason about the remaining leaks rigorously, we need a formally-grounded way to root-cause Spectre leakage in CTS* programs. Prior work (on hardware Spectre defenses) root-causes Spectre leakage of program secrets to access instructions, which load secrets into registers. However, placing a speculation fence—the only available ISA protection mechanism for blocking transient leakage—somewhere along every speculative control-flow path between every access instruction and every transmitter at compile time is not sufficient to prevent architecturally accessed secrets from transiently leaking.

Instead, we propose to root cause Spectre leakage program secrets to so-called taint primitives, which are instructions that can cause a publicly-typed register to transiently hold a secret. For example, a return instruction is a taint primitive on ASP hardware, because at its transient target, a register may be publicly-typed but hold secret data. We prove that taint primitives are necessary for Spectre leakage of secrets in CTS* programs.

1.3 The Serberus Defense

Putting together the solutions to these challenges and more, Serberus comprehensively secures CTS* programs against Spectre attacks using three compiler passes, which collectively eliminate all taint primitives from all of their (possible) transient executions. We have implemented these passes for LLVM. The function-private stacks pass assigns distinct stacks to each function in order to eliminate taint primitives that arise due to stack sharing. The register cleaning pass zeroes out registers at calls and returns to eliminate interprocedural taint primitives. The fence insertion pass inserts a minimal number of speculation fences to eliminate any taint primitives that the former two passes cannot handle.

We evaluated Serberus against an insecure baseline and two composite state-of-the-art defenses on a variety of cryptographic primitives from OpenSSL, Libsodium, and HACL*. Serberus exhibits 21.3% overhead across all benchmarks, and 7.1% overhead across benchmarks with larger inputs, compared to the insecure baseline. The latter is half the overhead of the next best defense, despite Serberus offering stronger security guarantees.

2 SynthLC: Push-Button Formal Verification of Hardware Leakage Contracts

SynthLC is the first automated approach and tool for formally verifying SystemVerilog processor implementations of nearly all state-of-the-art leakage contracts, including the constant-time leakage contract (adopted by industry as Arm DIT, Intel DOIT, and RISC-V Zkt) and more bespoke ones from academic research.[3] Beyond identifying (transmitter, unsafe-operand) pairs, like constant-time leakage contracts do, these bespoke contracts further detail the microarchitectural conditions under which transmitters leak their unsafe operands to improve the performance of hardware side-channel defenses that use them. The number and variety of proposed leakage contracts demonstrates significant progress in designing them, but less progress has been made toward verifying their correct implementation in hardware. SynthLC fills this leakage contract-microarchitecture verification gap as follows.

2.1 RTL2MμPATH Overview

First, SynthLC calls as a sub-routine RTL2MμPATH, another automated approach and tool we develop for synthesizing ("uncovering") a complete set of formally-verified microarchitectural execution paths (μPATHs) for each instruction as implemented on a SystemVerilog processor design. Each μPATH for an instruction (which we visualize as a directed acyclic graph) captures a partial happens-before order (directed edges) on the hardware events (nodes) associated with its execution in some reachable microarchitectural execution context on the design.

Given a SystemVerilog design under verification (DUV) and some modest design metadata as input, RTL2MμPATH considers one implemented instruction at a time, the instruction under verification (IUV). It first identifies an over-approximation of all μPATHs that the IUV could possibly take through the DUV. Then, it instantiates each μPATH possibility as a linear temporal logic property over DUV signals (expressed using SystemVerilog Assertion, or SVA, syntax) and directs a formal model checker to deduce its reachability. Reachable μPATHs are collected and unreachable μPATHs

---

[3] Yao Hsiao et al. "RTL2MμPATH: Multi-μPATH Synthesis with Applications to Hardware Security Verification". In: *Proceedings of the 57th IEEE/ACM International Symposium on Microarchitecture*. 2024.

are discarded. Importantly, a naïve over-approximation of all μPATHs for some IUV is proportional to the power set of all state elements in the DUV. RTL2MuPATH drastically reduces such an over-approximation to typically tens of (and at most about 1,000) μPATHs per IUV in our experiments using a novel conceptualization of μPATH nodes and a series of punning steps where it instantiate and model-checks auxiliary SVAs to avoid considering μPATHs that feature unreachable sub-μPATHs.

2.2 SynthLC Overview

In designing RTL2MuPATH, we observed that μPATH variability (>1 μPATH) for an instruction strongly indicates there is a hardware side-channel in the DUV.

For instance, a common hardware side-channel attack pattern involves a transmitter whose unsafe operand is supplied with secret data, and the transmitter creates and exhibits μPATH variability as a function of this operand. An example is a multiply transmitter on a processor that implements the zero-skip optimization, where multiplies exhibit a fast μPATH if at least one operand is zero and a slow μPATH otherwise. An attacker that can determine whether multiplies exhibit slow or fast μPATHs (e.g., by timing their execution) can learn whether their operands are both non-zero or not, respectively.

A more subtle hardware side-channel attack pattern involves a transmitter whose unsafe operand creates μPATH variability that is exhibited by a different dynamic instruction. For example, on the RISC-V processor that we use to evaluate RTL2MμPATH/SynthLC, a load can exhibit one of two distinct μPATHs—one where it stalls before accessing memory and another where it does not—depending on whether or not the page offset of the load's address operand matches that of any older pending store. Thus, a store transmitter that is supplied a secret address can leak this operand to an attacker that can distinguish stall versus non-stall μPATHs exhibited by other dynamic loads.

Based on our observation, SynthLC is an automated approach and tool that extends RTL2MμPATH with a symbolic information flow analysis, which again instantiates and model-checks SVAs, this time to synthesize a complete set of formally verified leakage signatures from a SystemVerilog processor design, assuming an attacker that can observe instruction/program execution time or resource contention. Each leakage signature precisely characterizes a hardware side-channel in the design, and a complete set of leakage signatures for a design captures all microarchitectural details required to implement the leakage contracts required by ten state-of-the-art hardware side-channel defenses.

3 Takeaways

In summary, this talk first presented Seberus, the first comprehensive Spectre-PHT/BTB/RSB/STL/PSF defense for constant-time, specifically CTS*, code that is deployable on existing hardware. Serberus is enabled by judiciously restricting a program's transitive control- and data-flow at compile time and by identifying taint primitives as the root-cause of Spectre leakage of secret data in CTS* code. Moreover,

Serberus shows that software Spectre defenses can be performant if they avoid fully disabling speculation. Serberus is open-source at https://github.com/nmosier/serberus.

Second, this talk introduced RTL2MμPATH and SynthLC, the first automated approaches and tools for synthesizing a complete set of formally-verified μPATHs and leakage signatures (characterizing all hardware side-channels), respectively, from an input SystemVerilog processor design. RTL2MμPATH/SynthLC automate SVA instantiation using pre-defined SVA property templates and static analysis of the design as well as analysis of the results of model-checking them. In designing both tools, we observed that μPATHs are a powerful microarchitectural intermediate representation for building formal verification procedures that assess hardware's adherence to leakage contracts (since transmitters create operand-dependent μPATH variability) and other important design specifications, which we are studying in follow-on work. This talk also introduced leakage signatures as a unifying formalism for capturing all state-of-the-art leakage contracts; thus, by synthesizing a complete set of formally-verified leakage signatures, SynthLC effectively synthesizes all of these leakage contracts as they are implemented in hardware. RTL2MμPATH/SynthLC are open-source at https://github.com/yaohsiaopid/SynthLC.

Tutorial

End-to-End Verification of Cryptographic Primitives with JASMIN and EASYCRYPT

Pierre-Yves Strub [ID]

PQShield
`pierre-yves.strub@pqshield.com`

Abstract. Cryptographic primitives are typically accompanied by rigorous security proofs at the level of abstract specifications, while their high-performance implementations are written and analyzed largely independently. This separation leaves room for subtle bugs that can invalidate security guarantees. In this tutorial, we present a layered formal verification approach for cryptographic primitives based on the combination of EASYCRYPT and JASMIN, developed within the Formosa project. EASYCRYPT is used to formalize and prove cryptographic security of specifications, as well as to verify functional correctness and memory safety of low-level implementations via extraction of JASMIN programs into EASYCRYPT . JASMIN enables the development of efficient, constant-time implementations and comes with a formally verified compiler. By linking verified implementations to secure specifications inside EASYCRYPT, security guarantees can be transported from abstract models to concrete code. This approach supports end-to-end, machine-checked assurance for efficient cryptographic primitives.

Keywords: Formal verification · Cryptographic primitives · EASYCRYPT · JASMIN · Constant-time programming · Functional correctness · Memory safety · Verified compilation.

Cryptographic primitives form the foundation of modern secure systems. Their correctness and security are critical: flaws at this level can compromise entire protocols and applications, even when higher-level designs are sound. Many real-world failures stem not from broken mathematics, but from mismatches between a proven-secure design and what actually runs, including implementation bugs, memory errors, or side-channel leakage.

Traditionally, assurance splits along a fault line. Cryptographers prove the security of *abstract specifications* under precise adversarial models. Implementers write fast low-level code (often hand-optimized) and attempt to enforce constant-time discipline and avoid undefined behavior. The gap between these artifacts is where vulnerabilities thrive: a security proof about a specification does not automatically apply to a particular implementation, and confidence in low-level code does not imply cryptographic security.

Formal verification offers a way to close this gap. However, it must address heterogeneous reasoning problems: probabilistic relational reasoning for cryptographic security, functional correctness and memory safety for low-level code, and non-functional security properties such as constant-timeness. EASYCRYPT and JASMIN, developed within the

Formosa project, together support a layered verification approach for high-performance cryptographic primitives.

1 Three Layers of Verification

Cryptographic Security of Specifications. At the top layer, cryptographic primitives are described by mathematical specifications. Security is expressed using game-based or simulation-based definitions comparing a *real* construction to an *ideal* one. These arguments are probabilistic and relational, quantify over adversaries, and often rely on subtle game transformations, making them well-suited to mechanized verification.

Full Correctness of High-Speed Implementations. The second layer establishes that an optimized implementation computes the specified function and does so safely. For cryptographic primitives, the key properties include:

- *Functional correctness*: outputs match the intended specification for all inputs.
- *Memory safety*: no out-of-bounds accesses, no misuse of stack or heap regions, and no undefined behaviors in the modeled semantics.

This layer is indispensable: a single arithmetic error, incorrect carry propagation, or memory bug can invalidate security claims or introduce exploitable vulnerabilities.

Security of Implementations. The third layer captures implementation-level security properties not implied by functional correctness, most prominently *constant-timeness*. Constant-time guarantees aim to prevent timing and microarchitectural side channels by ensuring that control flow and memory access patterns do not depend on secret data.

Ultimately, all three layers must be composed: a secure specification, a correct and safe implementation of that specification, and evidence that the implementation does not leak secrets via side channels.

2 EASYCRYPT: Proving Cryptographic Security of Specifications

EASYCRYPT[4] is a proof assistant tailored to cryptography. It supports probabilistic programming, adversary modeling, and relational logics that make it natural to formalize security definitions and game-based proofs. EASYCRYPT enables structured proofs of indistinguishability, advantage bounds, and reductions, while ensuring that all reasoning steps are machine-checked.

Within the Formosa toolchain, EASYCRYPT plays a dual role. First, it is the environment in which cryptographic security of abstract specifications is formalized and proved. Second, it is the environment in which functional correctness and memory safety of low-level implementations are verified, via extraction of JASMIN programs into EASYCRYPT.

Beyond these core uses, EASYCRYPT provides a rich standard library of cryptographic primitives, probabilistic distributions, and algebraic theories, which facilitates

---

[4] https://www.easycrypt.info/.

modular and reusable developments. Its support for *relational program logics*, such as probabilistic relational Hoare logic (pRHL), allows one to reason about relationships between multiple program executions.

EASYCRYPT also supports a game-hopping methodology, where security proofs are structured as a sequence of small, justified transformations between games. Each hop is accompanied by a formally verified argument, such as program equivalence or bounded difference, making the overall proof both robust and auditable. This methodology aligns closely with pen-and-paper cryptographic proofs, easing the transition from informal arguments to fully mechanized ones.

3 JASMIN: High-Performance Low-Level Code with a Verified Compiler

JASMIN[5] is an *assembly-in-the-head* programming language designed for writing high-speed cryptographic code while remaining compatible with formal reasoning. It provides explicit control over registers, memory layout, and low-level operations, within a structured language equipped with a precise formal semantics. This design allows developers to write code that closely reflects the intended assembly-level behavior, while remaining amenable to formal analysis and verification.

A key feature of JASMIN is its focus on security-critical properties that are essential for cryptographic implementations. In particular, the language enforces a disciplined programming model that facilitates constant-time programming, helping to prevent timing and microarchitectural side-channel attacks. The explicit handling of state and memory makes data dependencies transparent, which is crucial for both performance optimization and security reasoning.

JASMIN comes with a formally verified compiler that translates JASMIN programs into target-specific assembly code. The correctness of this compilation process is proved with respect to the formal semantics of the language, ensuring that the generated assembly faithfully implements the behavior of the source program. This provides a high-assurance path from verified source code to executable binaries, reducing the trusted computing base of cryptographic software.

JASMIN occupies a middle ground between handwritten assembly and high-level languages: it is low-level enough to enable tight, performance-oriented and constant-time implementations, yet structured enough to support rigorous verification. In particular, JASMIN programs can be connected to higher-level specifications and proofs, for instance through integration with the EASYCRYPT proof assistant. This positioning makes JASMIN a key component in end-to-end verification toolchains that aim to deliver cryptographic implementations that are both efficient and provably secure.

---

[5] https://github.com/jasmin-lang/jasmin.

4 From JASMIN to EASYCRYPT

Memory safety and functional correctness of JASMIN programs are established within the EASYCRYPT proof assistant, using an extraction pipeline that reifies JASMIN code into EASYCRYPT . This design enables low-level implementations to be reasoned about within the same formal framework as cryptographic specifications, while keeping the proof obligations associated with different concerns clearly separated.

The extraction process translates a JASMIN program into an EASYCRYPT model that captures the program's operational behavior, including registers, memory, arithmetic, and control flow. Memory safety is addressed directly at this level of abstraction. The extracted semantics makes all memory accesses explicit, enabling formal proofs that every read and write operation remains within allocated regions and respects the intended memory layout. A significant part of these proof obligations are discharged automatically by the JASMIN extractor. Discharging the remaining, more complex, obligations ensures that the JASMIN program is safe according to its formal semantics.

Once cryptographic security has been established for an abstract specification, and safety properties have been proved for a corresponding JASMIN implementation, the final step is to connect the two so that the security guarantees carry over to the implementation. This connection is naturally expressed within EASYCRYPT, since both the specification and the extracted implementation are available in the same logical environment. Functional correctness is then proved by relating the extracted JASMIN semantics to a reference functional specification. Concretely, one shows in EASYCRYPT that, for all inputs satisfying the preconditions, executing the JASMIN program produces outputs equal to those of the reference specification.

This overall structure avoids the need to re-prove cryptographic security at the level of low-level code and supports a clean separation of concerns, while still providing end-to-end, machine-checked assurance from specification to implementation.

5 Verifying Constant-Timeness with JASMIN

Beyond functional correctness, JASMIN supports verification of *constant-time* properties, which are crucial for resistance against timing-based and microarchitectural side-channel attacks. The language design makes control flow, data dependencies, and memory accesses fully explicit, allowing precise analyses that ensure secret data does not influence branch conditions or memory access patterns. As a result, one can formally state and prove that executions with different secret inputs are indistinguishable with respect to their observable timing behavior.

These constant-time properties are verified at the level of the JASMIN semantics, using dedicated analyses and proof techniques that reason about information flow and control-flow. The explicit structure of JASMIN programs simplifies the formulation of these proofs and enables a high degree of automation, reducing the manual effort required to establish side-channel resistance.

Contents

Rely-Guarantee Verification of Queue Locks with Proof Support in Isabelle/HOL

Robert J. Colvin[1,2], Scott Heiner[2], Peter Höfner[3], and Roger C. Su[3(✉)]

[1] Defence Science and Technology Group, Brisbane, Australia
[2] University of Queensland, Brisbane, Australia
{r.colvin,s.heiner}@uq.edu.au
[3] Australian National University, Canberra, Australia
peter.hoefner@anu.edu.au, roger.c.su@proton.me

Abstract. To support rely-guarantee reasoning, we present an extension to Isabelle/HOL's built-in library, which we use to verify a hierarchy of queue locks. The framework incorporates novel features of Isabelle, and enables flexible syntax, assertion-annotations, and tactics for both automated and structured proofs. Assertion-annotations enable elegant top-down specification from an abstract queue lock to a non-trivial, practical circular-buffer queue lock.

1 Introduction

Concurrent systems are deeply integrated in the society, encompassing many safety critical systems, such as automotive, aviation, and medical devices. Reasoning about these systems is challenging, especially when considering the interference between the individual *threads* that share resources and information.

Rely-guarantee (RG) reasoning, first developed in 1983 by Jones [13], provides a formal, compositional framework to reason about such interference. Each thread *guarantees* a certain behaviour, but only when it can *rely* on its *environment* (i.e. all other threads) to maintain an acceptable level of interference. The rely- and guarantee-conditions form a contract, allowing a large, complex system to be decomposed into smaller components. One can then reason about each component separately, through the component's own rely-guarantee contract.

RG reasoning is based on Hoare triples, which feature a precondition, a command, and a postcondition. It augments the precondition with a rely condition, and the postcondition with a guarantee condition, resulting in a *quintuple*. A formulation of RG was mechanised in Isabelle/HOL by Prensa Nieto [18] in 2003. Since then, Isabelle/HOL [16] has improved considerably, with advances such as the automation tool Sledgehammer [3] being released in 2011, and the tactics language Eisbach [15] in 2016. We modernise and enhance this library.

To allow for understandable and maintainable specifications, we develop flexible syntax on top of the built-in RG library to support both the 'quintuple style' and the 'VDM keyword style' of RG specification. We also enable one to factor

C. Pit-Claudel and K. Kosaian (Eds.): VSTTE 2025, LNCS 16499, pp. 1–19, 2026.
https://doi.org/10.1007/978-3-032-27340-6_1

out a shared *data-invariant*, which would otherwise need to be repeated across the specification. Additionally we extend the syntax of commands to include embedded *annotations* (assertions). We develop novel tactics that support both automated and structured proof styles, and take advantage of annotations to discharge many trivial side conditions. All of these aim to make the specifications and proofs easier to develop and maintain. The syntax and tactics have been applied to a variety of case studies, including the examples in the built-in Isabelle library, as well as a hierarchy of queue locks; on the former, our syntax and tactics greatly simplify their proofs and improves their readability. Our source files are publicly available and ready to be used by others [7].

Outline. Section 2 recalls the relevant background on Isabelle/HOL. Section 3 then covers the basics of RG reasoning, while presenting our syntax extensions. Section 4 introduces the enhanced RG inference rules and our tactics. Section 5 specifies and verifies the Abstract Queue Lock. Sections 6 and 7 provide more complex examples of a Ticket Lock and a Circular-Buffer Lock. Section 8 provides directions for future work and concludes.

1.1   Related Work

Mechanised Rely-Guarantee. We are not aware of any work that builds on Isabelle/HOL's built-in RG library [18], except for our earlier work [5], which motivated us to extend the library more systematically.

CSimpl [21] and CSim2 [22] are RG verification frameworks in Isabelle/HOL. They derive from the sequential-programming framework Simpl [23], which supports exception-handling and aborting behaviour, among others. These extra functionalities come at a cost of high complexity in the logic. In many verification cases (such as the ones presented in this paper), the programs of interest do not involve these extra functionalities, and are thus better suited to a more lightweight framework. Compared to those works, our framework also supports command annotations, which contribute to better usability. (Simpl has also been extended to concurrency by Complx [1], which does not use RG reasoning.)

RG has been mechanised in Rocq (formerly Coq) by Zakowski et al. [25], who based the logic on an intermediate representation language, and employed it to verify a concurrent garbage collector. We chose to use Isabelle/HOL in order to leverage its automated tools (e.g. Sledgehammer) and its structured proof language. Another formulation of RG is the algebraic style of Hayes et al. [6,9], where relies, guarantees, preconditions, postconditions, and commands are all elements of an algebra. This style of RG, however, is not yet ready for practical applications, as its foundations are still being updated recently [10].

Locks. The background and history of locks are widely discussed in the literature (e.g., [11,19]), and there have been works that use various logics and tools to verify different locks. For example, the Bakery Algorithm was verified with PVS [12], the MCS Lock was verified using the 'certified concurrent abstraction layers' methodology [14], and the CLH Lock was verified with custom-built program logics [20,24]. In comparison, we verify locks with the rely-guarantee logic in Isabelle/HOL, and thus demonstrate another technique for concurrency verification. Moreover, we present the locks hierarchically from abstract to concrete, showing how our methodology can be applied to other locks and even other concurrent data structures.

2   Isabelle/HOL

The definitions and theorems in this paper are implemented in the interactive proof assistant Isabelle/HOL [16], and is available on the Archive of Formal Proofs [7]. In this section, we introduce the relevant basics, using the Abstract Queue Lock as a running example.

In Isabelle/HOL, common basic types include `nat` and `bool`. Type-variables are prefixed with apostrophes (`'a`). Functions from `'a` to `'b` have type `'a ⇒ 'b`. The symbol `o>` denotes forward function-composition: `(f o> g) x = g (f x)`.

New types can be defined using the keywords **type_synonym** and **datatype**. When specifying locks, we identify individual threads using the type `thread_id`, which we define as: **type_synonym** `thread_id = nat`.

For parametric types, the type parameters are written *before* the type constructors. In particular, `'a list` denotes the type of lists, where `#` denotes the *cons* operation that adds an element to the front of a list, and `@` denotes list-concatenation. Other common parametric types include sets (`'a set`), relations (**type_synonym** `'a rel = ('a × 'a) set`), and the option-type (**datatype** `'a option = None | Some 'a`).

We further define the following two notions. The abbreviation `at_head` describes when 'an element `x` is at the head of a list `ys`'. Note that both clauses must be present in `at_head` to characterise the predicate faithfully, because the term `x = hd ys` (`x` being the head of `ys`) does not imply `x ∈ set ys` in Isabelle/HOL. The notion `pred_to_rel` lifts a predicate `p` (encoded as a set) to a relation, in which `p` being true in the pre-state implies that `p` is true in the post-state.

```
abbreviation at_head x ys ≡ x ∈ set ys ∧ x = hd ys
definition pred_to_rel p ≡ {(s,s'). s ∈ p ⟶ s' ∈ p}
```

2.1   Records

New types with multiple fields can be defined using the keyword **record**, which is used in this paper to model the states of concurrent programs. For example, the state of the Abstract Queue Lock is defined as:

```
record queue_lock = queue :: thread_id list
```

This definition introduces a new type `queue_lock`, with a single field `queue`, which corresponds to a function of type `queue_lock ⇒ thread_id list`.

The built-in RG library further defines the following specialised set-builder notations, which are often used on records.

(1) The acute symbol ($´$) abbreviates certain function applications in a set-builder expression. For example, $\{\!|$ `distinct` $´$`queue` $\wedge$ `length` $´$`queue` `< 5` $|\!\}$ is equivalent to `{x. distinct (queue x)` $\wedge$ `length (queue x) < 5}`.

This notation is not just for the fields of a record type, but also for any function on the record type. Moreover, there can be multiple different functions prefixed by the acute symbol within one pair of double braces.

(2) For set-builder expressions describing relations, the symbols ^{o} and ^{a} denote variables of the pre-state (the *old*-state) and the post-state (the *after*-state). For example, the following two expressions are equivalent:

```
{| length °queue < length ªqueue |}
{ (x1, x2). length (queue x1) < length (queue x2) }
```

This notation, ^{o}x and ^{a}x, corresponds to the standard RG-notation x and x$'$.

3   Rely-Guarantee Reasoning

Developed by Jones [13], the rely-guarantee (RG) reasoning paradigm augments a Hoare triple with a *rely* and a *guarantee*, which are relations on states and describe the allowed interaction between a thread and its *environment* (i.e. all other threads that run in parallel). A thread requires every environment-step to satisfy the rely, and if so, each step of the thread would uphold the guarantee.

A basic sentence in RG is a quintuple that consists of a precondition `P` (a set of states), a rely-relation `R` (a relation on states), a program/command `c` (of type `'a com`), a guarantee-relation `G` (a relation on states), a postcondition `Q` (a set of states). If `c` starts in a state satisfying `P` and each step of the environment satisfies `R`, then `c` will finish in a state satisfying `Q`, with each transition satisfying `G`. Collectively, `P`, `R`, `G`, and `Q` are called the *specification components*.

In the original library [18], an RG sentence is written as

$$\vdash \texttt{c sat [P, R, G, Q]} \ .$$

In our syntax extension, a basic RG sentence is written `rely: R guar: G code:` `{P} c {Q}`, or more concisely

$$\texttt{\{P,R\} c \{G,Q\}} \ .$$

These are closer to the common notation used in the RG literature.

The original library defines commands using a simple while-language; the type `'a com` encompasses sequential commands that act on states of type `'a`. A parallel composition combines sequential commands in a list. Annotations will be defined in Sect. 3.2.

3.1 Data-Invariant

Often, all four specification components contain a common *data-invariant* I that can be factored out. Such an RG sentence with six components is written as (1) or (2) below, both of which abbreviate (3).

```
(1)   {P,R} c ∥ I {G,Q}
(2)   rely: R guar: G inv: I code: { P } c { Q }
(3)   {P ∩ I, R ∩ pred_to_rel I} c {G ∩ pred_to_rel I, Q ∩ I}
```

Here, `pred_to_rel` lifts the predicate from set to relation, as defined just before Sect. 2.1. This syntactic sugar makes specifications more concise by avoiding replication of what is often a long expression, thus minimising translation errors.

3.2 Annotated Commands

When reasoning about programs, it is common and useful practice to interleave assertions amid instructions, which illustrates more clearly how the individual instructions affect the state and how they interact (e.g. [1,17]). The commands (`'a com`) in the original library do not allow for such annotations of assertions, so we define the new type *annotated commands* (`'a anncom`), whose main cases are listed and explained below.[1]

```
datatype 'a anncom = NoAnno 'a com | BasicAnno  'a ⇒ 'a
  | SeqAnno      'a anncom 'a set     'a anncom
  | CondAnno     'a bexp   'a anncom 'a anncom
  | WhileAnno    'a bexp   'a set     'a anncom
  | ...
```

The constructor `NoAnno` directly wraps a non-annotated command. Meanwhile, `BasicAnno f` abbreviates `NoAnno (Basic f)`, where `(Basic f)` is a non-annotated command that encodes the state-transformation function `f`, which models `SKIP`, single assignments, and multiple assignments. Multiple assignments (used in Sects. 6 and 7) are performed in a single step, by combining them with function-composition and wrapping the resultant function in a Basic instruction. Such a 'multi-assignment' is used to couple auxiliary instructions with concrete instructions, or to model RMW instructions such as fetch-and-increment.

In a sequential composition of two commands (`SeqAnno c1 p c2`), the intermediate assertion `p` serves as the postcondition of `c1` and the precondition of `c2`, thus transforming the overall proof goal into two subgoals.

The if-then-else construct (`CondAnno`) consists of a Boolean expression as the guard, and two annotated commands as the then-branch and the else-branch. As for the while-loop (`WhileAnno`), the Boolean expression is the guard, the set represents an assertion for the state after the guard but before the loop's body, which is the annotated command. A typical RG sentence on annotated commands is

---

[1] The type-variable `'a` is to be instantiated with the state.

6   R. J. Colvin et al.

written: {P, R} c {G, Q}, and the notation for data-invariants is supported similarly as in Sect. 3.1, except that the invariant is pushed through the syntactic structure to be included in the annotations.

A parallel composition is defined as a list of annotated commands. The annotated commands in such a list often have the same form, as in the examples of locks later in this paper. For this type of parallel composition, we express its specification using the *multi-parallel* sentence below. Let P, R, G, and Q be the precondition, rely, guarantee, and postcondition of the 'global' parallel composition. Furthermore, the parallel composition consists of n threads, where each thread i has precondition P i, rely R i, annotated command c i, guarantee G i, and postcondition Q i. The multi-parallel sentence is then written as follows:

```
annotated  global_init: P  global_rely: R
   ‖ i < n @
{P i, R i} c i {G i, Q i}
global_guar: G  global_post: Q
```

The global specification components allow the parallel composition to be embedded into a wider context, thus enabling compositional reasoning.

3.3   Example (Specification of Abstract Queue Lock)

We now demonstrate the use of annotated commands and their RG sentences (Sect. 3.2), by specifying parts of the Abstract Queue Lock. The full specification of the Abstract Queue Lock will be completed later in Sect. 5.

A lock is a synchronisation mechanism to ensure that only one thread at a time can enter its 'critical section' of code and access a shared resource. Before a thread enters its critical section, it must first *acquire* the lock; if the lock is already held by another thread, the acquiring thread waits until the lock becomes available. Once the thread has finished executing its critical section, it *releases* the lock, allowing other threads to acquire it.

The Abstract Queue Lock manages access to the critical section by a shared queue to guarantee the *first-in first-served* property. The command acquire consists of two steps: joining the queue, and checking whether it has reached the head of the queue. As soon as the thread is at the head of the queue, it has successfully acquired the lock. This corresponds to the following two commands.[2]

```
´queue := ´queue @ [t]    ;   WHILE (hd ´queue ≠ t) DO SKIP OD
```

The loop of the second command, which contains the empty body, is referred to as a *spinloop*. Thread t is said to *spin* on the value hd ´queue ≠ t.

The acquire command should only be invoked by Thread t when it is not already holding or queueing for the lock. This means that the precondition of

---

[2] The record-field queue acts on an underlying state, so the acute symbol is needed to represent this hidden function application (see Sect. 2.1).

acquire, invoked by Thread t, is ⦃ t ∉ set ´queue ⦄. After the first instruction, t becomes a part of the queue, but is not necessarily at the head; hence, the intermediate assertion is ⦃ t ∈ set ´queue ⦄. After t finishes executing acquire, it will be at the head of the queue (and, by definition, holding the lock); hence, the postcondition is ⦃ at_head t ´queue ⦄.

Furthermore, each thread should only acquire the lock one at a time. That means that each thread should only occur at most once in the queue, which is formalised by the data-invariant ⦃ distinct ´queue ⦄– see Sect. 3.1. Suppose for now that the rely and guarantee of acquire are R and G respectively. Then, the RG sentence for acquire is written as follows, after combining the annotated command with the pre- and postconditions.[3]

```
rely: R  guar: G  inv: ⦃ distinct ´queue ⦄
anno_code:
   ⦃ t ∉ set ´queue ⦄
NoAnno ( ´queue :=  ´queue @ [t]) .;
   ⦃ t ∈ set ´queue ⦄
NoAnno (WHILE hd ´queue ≠ t DO SKIP OD)
   ⦃ at_head t ´queue ⦄
```

Our proof assistance includes further syntactic sugar to simplify the presentation of annotated commands, but we omit that in this paper for clarity.

4   Inference Rules and Tactics

We now turn to the inference rules on RG sentences involving our extended syntax. Based on these inference rules, we then define our tactics, which support both *structured* and *semi-automatic* approaches to theorem-proving.

4.1   Inference Rules

We summarise the subset of RG inference rules we apply in this paper. RG reasoning requires that every pre- and postcondition in a proof is stable under environment interference: a set (predicate) S is *stable* under a transition relation R, if the post-state x' satisfies S, whenever the pre-state satisfies S.

```
definition stable :: 'a set ⇒ 'a rel ⇒ bool where
   stable S R ≡ ∀ x x' . x ∈ S ∧ (x, x') ∈ R ⟶ x' ∈ S
```

Our first rule is on Basic instructions, which encompass single or multiple assignments, SKIP, and state-transformations in general. To guarantee non-interference from the environment, the pre- and postconditions need to be stable under the rely. If the start state is in P, then f should result in a state in Q. The guarantee should contain the identity-relation restricted to P; this accounts for

---

[3] We have omitted some brackets to improve readability.

the possibility of the current thread not taking any step. Meanwhile, the state transformation f needs to uphold the guarantee as well.

$$\frac{\begin{array}{cc} \texttt{stable P R} \quad \texttt{stable Q R} \quad \texttt{P} \subseteq \{\![\ \text{`}\texttt{f} \in \texttt{Q}]\!\} \\ \forall \texttt{s.}\ \texttt{s} \in \texttt{P} \longrightarrow (\texttt{s, s}) \in \texttt{G} \qquad \forall \texttt{s.}\ \texttt{s} \in \texttt{P} \longrightarrow (\texttt{s, f s}) \in \texttt{G} \end{array}}{\texttt{\{P,R\} Basic f \{G,Q\}}} \text{ (basic)}$$

The rule for spinloops is a specialised version of the original rule for WHILE. As before, the pre- and postconditions must be stable under the rely. The guarantee must contain the identity-relation restricted to P; however, as a spinloop changes nothing, we can assume that the guarantee contains the full identity relation. Finally, if a state satisfies the precondition but not the guard, then we exit the spinloop, and the same state must satisfy the postcondition.

$$\frac{\texttt{stable P R} \quad \texttt{stable Q R} \quad \texttt{Id} \subseteq \texttt{G} \quad \texttt{P} \cap \texttt{-b} \subseteq \texttt{Q}}{\texttt{\{P,R\} WHILE b DO SKIP OD \{G,Q\}}} \text{ (spinloop)}$$

The two rules above involve non-annotated commands, as Basic commands and spinloops do not need annotations in practice. The annotated version of all the existing RG rules [4] can be implemented in our framework, including the well-known rule for sequential composition, where M is the 'middle' assertion.

$$\frac{\texttt{\{P,R\} ac1 \{G,M\}} \quad \texttt{\{M,R\} ac2 \{G,Q\}}}{\texttt{\{P,R\} ac1 ; \{M\} ac2 \{G,Q\}}} \text{ (seq)}$$

This rule demonstrates the usefulness of annotated commands. In contrast to the original, non-annotated version, we can now explicitly characterise the mid-state as part of the RG sentence. All other rules—such as the two-branch if-block, one-branch if-block, and infinite loop—can be found in our source files [7].

4.2   Tactics

In interactive proof assistants, a *tactic* (or *method*) is a procedure that transforms proof goals in an attempt to solve them (semi-)automatically; either the goal is solved entirely, or some (simpler) subgoals remain.

Tactics in Isabelle/HOL were historically written in the ML programming language, which requires detailed understanding of ML and the internals of Isabelle/HOL. The Eisbach language [15] abstracts many of these advanced, ML-level features into high-level constructs in Isabelle/HOL's input language, thus allowing for easier and more natural specification of tactics. Tactics in Eisbach are defined using the same syntax as proofs. For example,

`method conj_solver = (rule conjI; assumption)`

defines a tactic `conj_solver` that attempts to resolve a conjunction automatically. It uses the *structured concatenation* combinator (;), which applies the method `assumption` to all subgoals that emerge from the application of the rule `conjI`.

We defined around ten different tactics in Eisbach. Here we only describe the ones we regularly use in our case-studies.

Our main tactic, `rg_anno_ultimate`, is based on the inference rules on annotated commands. It tries to apply all possible inference rules, and when it succeeds, it generates the appropriate proof skeleton. This tactic is vital during the development process, as the structured proof skeleton lets us easily identify any missing lemma or any error in the specification.

After applications of `rg_anno_ultimate`, we reach RG sentences on the indivisible `Basic` commands and spinloops. Here, we apply the tactics `method_basic` or `method_spinloop`. These basic tactics can generate proof skeletons according to the rules in Sect. 4.1; in simpler cases, they can be combined with built-in automatic tactics (such as `fastforce`) using the structured concatenation combinator (;) to discharge the goal in one line.

Tactics with Higher Automation. The tactics above are mainly aimed for the structured style of proofs. In the automated style, our tactic `rg_proof_expand` eagerly simplifies an RG sentence and its subgoals, using Isabelle/HOL's built-in automated reasoners. This tactic first applies the built-in `auto` tactic, while restricting its rule-set to a collection of RG-related lemmas—including the RG inference rules and their alternative formulations. This phase decomposes all the RG sentences into proof obligations, on which the tactic then invokes the built-in simplifier `simp`.

The automated tactic `rg_proof_expand` is useful when the specification has been finalised, and when the program of interest does not require many additional lemmas—such as the 'findP' program, which is a standard example in concurrency verification. The findP program involves n threads that concurrently search in an array for an entry satisfying some predicate P. Specifically, each thread i searches only the array-entries whose indices are congruent to i mod n.

This program was verified in the original RG library, with a proof that consists of more than 25 apply-commands, including many manual choices of primitive rules and manual instantiations of rules.

Our proof below is systematic and many side conditions are automatically discharged. The application of `rg_proof_expand` leaves us ten subgoals that purely involve list-indexing and could not be discharged by `simp` alone. The first seven subgoals are discharged by the standard method `force`. Isabelle/HOL automatically finds the proofs of the final three subgoals, using the Sledgehammer tool [3].

```
apply rg_proof_expand
        apply force+
  apply (metis linorder_neqE_nat mod_aux)
  apply (metis antisym_conv3 mod_aux)
by (metis leD mod_less_eq_dividend)
```

5   Abstract Queue Lock

We now pick up from Sect. 3.3, and complete the specification of the Abstract Queue Lock. We discuss the correctness properties, the rely and guarantee, and the main RG theorem. These discussions in this abstract setting will later guide us in formalising the specifications of the Ticket Lock and Circular Buffer Lock.

As discussed earlier, the main data structure of this lock is a queue, modelled as a list in Isabelle/HOL. Each thread that wishes to enter the critical section joins at the end of the list and leaves from its head. In a queue, each element can occur at most once. Hence, the data-invariant is expressed as the set of states where the queue contains distinct elements: ⦃ `distinct` `queue` ⦄.

We view a thread as holding the lock if and only if that thread is at the head of the queue. As a queue has at most one unique head, this modelling choice directly upholds the *mutual exclusion property*—that 'the lock is held by at most one thread at a time'. (We omit the critical section, which we assume not to modify any variable of the lock.)

Contract (Rely and Guarantee). There are other desirable properties of locks that are described in terms of the interaction between a thread and its environment.

When Thread `i` holds the lock, the lock cannot be taken away by the environment, and only `i` itself can release the lock; we call this the *self-releasing property*. In the context of queue locks, this translates to the statement *head stays at the head*.

The concurrent system of a lock is symmetric in that every thread has the same behaviour. This symmetry enables the rely and the guarantee to be described by a common relation, which we term the *contract*. Thread `i` relies on its contract being met, and guarantees to respect the contracts of all other threads. The latter can be expressed in terms of the `for_others` function below. It takes an indexed relation `r`, where `r i` in our context represents the contract of Thread `i`. Now, `for_others r i` is defined below as the intersection of all other threads' contracts `r j`, where `j ≠ i`. This relation is what Thread `i` must guarantee.

```
abbreviation for_others :: ('i ⇒ 's rel) ⇒ 'i ⇒ 's rel where
  for_others r i ≡ ⋂ j∈-{ i }. r j
```

Overall, the following is the contract of the Abstract Queue Lock. The first clause states that a thread cannot be added to or removed from the queue by its environment. The second clause states that the *head stays at the head*. Both are classical rely-conditions.[4]

```
abbreviation queue_contract :: thread_id ⇒ queue_lock rel where
  queue_contract i ≡ ⦃ (i ∈ set ᵒqueue ⟷ i ∈ set ᵃqueue)
                      ∧ (at_head i ᵒqueue ⟶ at_head i ᵃqueue) ⦄
```

---

[4] Recall the special small-o and small-a notation from the end of Sect. 2.1.

Theorems. On the top-level, each thread repeatedly uses the lock in the pattern `WHILE True DO (acquire ; release) OD`. We omit the critical section between `acquire` and `release`, as it does not access the lock. In the body of the infinite loop, `acquire` consists of two steps, enqueuing and spinning, while `release` consists only of the single dequeuing step. The local invariant, assertions, and contract are as presented earlier.

The top-level RG sentence is hence the global parallel theorem below. The queue is initially empty. Since there is no other actor outside of the collection of threads, the rely is the identity relation (no external interference) and the guarantee is the universal relation (all variables are potentially modified). Finally, because the outer loop never terminates (a continuously executing system), the global postcondition is left as the trivial empty set.

```
theorem qlock_global: assumes 0 < n shows
  annotated  global_init: { ´queue = [] }  global_rely: Id
    || i < n @ { i ∉ set ´queue }, queue_contract i
  WHILE True DO  {stable_guard: { i ∉ set ´queue } }
    NoAnno ( ´queue := ´queue @ [i]) .;
      { i ∈ set ´queue }
    NoAnno (WHILE hd ´queue ≠ i DO SKIP OD) .;
      { at_head i ´queue }
    NoAnno ( ´queue := tl ´queue) OD // { distinct ´queue }
  { for_others queue_contract i, {} }
  global_guar: UNIV  global_post: {}
```

For this relatively simple program, our automated tactic `rg_proof_expand` transforms this theorem into four subgoals. Among these, the first three subgoals are RG sentences corresponding to the three instructions inside the infinite loop. Note that `rg_proof_expand` decomposes the global parallel sentence into the infinite loop, and then decomposes the infinite loop into its three constituent instructions, while discharging most of the side-condition checks automatically. Now, the first two RG sentences can be discharged by single lines, while the last RG sentence can be resolved in a separate lemma using a structured proof (see our source files [7] for more detail). The final small subgoal can also be discharged automatically. These result in the following five-line proof.

```
apply rg_proof_expand
    apply (method_rg_basic_named; fastforce)
  apply (method_spinloop; fastforce)
  using qlock_rel apply fastforce
using assms by fastforce
```

6   Ticket Lock

We now specify the Ticket Lock as an implementation of the Abstract Queue Lock. The state of the Ticket Lock consists of three fields:

(1) `myticket :: thread_id ⇒ nat`,
(2) `now_serving :: nat`, and
(3) `next_ticket :: nat`.

Every thread locally stores a ticket number, and this collection of local variables is modelled globally by the `myticket` function. When Thread `i` joins the queue, it sets `myticket i` to be the value `next_ticket`, and atomically increments `next_ticket`; this corresponds to the atomic Fetch-And-Add instruction, which is supported on most computer systems. Thread `i` then waits until the `now_serving` value becomes equal to its own ticket number `myticket i`. When Thread `i` leaves the queue, it increments `now_serving`.

This corresponds to the following code for `acquire` and `release`. Note that we use forward function composition to model the Fetch-And-Add atomic block.

```
acquire ≡ ((myticket i := next_ticket) o>
             (next_ticket := next_ticket + 1)) ;
           WHILE now_serving ≠ myticket i DO SKIP OD)


release ≡ now_serving := now_serving + 1
```

Conceptually, Thread `i` is in the queue if and only if `now_serving` ≤ `myticket i`, and is at the head if and only if `now_serving` = `myticket i`.

6.1   Invariant

We now formalise the invariant of the Ticket Lock. The first three clauses are inequalities, while the last two clauses will be explained in more detail below.

```
abbreviation tktlock_inv ≡ {| ´now_serving ≤ ´next_ticket
  ∧ (1 ≤ ´now_serving) ∧ (∀ i. ´myticket i < ´next_ticket)
  ∧ bij_betw ´myticket ´tktlock_contending_set
                    {´now_serving ..< ´next_ticket}
  ∧ inj_img ´myticket positive_nats |}
```

The predicate `bij_betw f A B` holds if and only if `f` is bijective when its domain is restricted to `A` and its codomain restricted to `B`. The penultimate clause of the invariant stipulates that for every valid state `s`, the function `myticket s` is bijective between the set of queuing/contending threads (those threads whose tickets are not smaller than `now_serving`) and the set of tickets in use (those numbers from `now_serving` up to, but not including `next_ticket`). In the final clause of the invariant, `inj_img f B` holds if and only if `f` is injective when its codomain is restricted to `B`. Hence, the final clause of the invariant ensures that the function `myticket s` is injective when 0 is excluded from its codomain. In other words, all threads, whose tickets are non-zero, hold unique tickets.

6.2 Contract

The contract of the ticket lock, `tktlock_contract` below, describes the expected behaviour of the environment. The first clause ensures that the local variable `myticket i` does not change. Meanwhile, the global variables `next_ticket` and `now_serving` must not decrease, which is described by the second and third clause of `tktlock_contract`.

The last two clauses of `tktlock_contract` correspond to the two clauses of the contract of the Abstract Queue Lock, where `i ∈ set queue` and `at_head i queue` under the Abstract Queue Lock respectively translate to `now_serving ≤ myticket i` and `now_serving = myticket i` under the Ticket Lock.

$$
\begin{aligned}
&\textbf{abbreviation } \texttt{tktlock\_contract i} \equiv \{\!| \ ^{\text{\O}}\texttt{myticket i} = {}^{\text{a}}\texttt{myticket i} \\
&\quad \wedge \ ^{\text{\O}}\texttt{next\_ticket} \leq {}^{\text{a}}\texttt{next\_ticket} \ \wedge \ ^{\text{\O}}\texttt{now\_serving} \leq {}^{\text{a}}\texttt{now\_serving} \\
&\quad \wedge \ (^{\text{\O}}\texttt{now\_serving} \leq {}^{\text{\O}}\texttt{myticket i} \longleftrightarrow {}^{\text{a}}\texttt{now\_serving} \leq {}^{\text{a}}\texttt{myticket i}) \\
&\quad \wedge \ (^{\text{\O}}\texttt{now\_serving} = {}^{\text{\O}}\texttt{myticket i} \longrightarrow {}^{\text{a}}\texttt{now\_serving} = {}^{\text{a}}\texttt{myticket i}) \ |\!\}
\end{aligned}
$$

6.3 RG Theorems

Similar to the Abstract Queue Lock, the specification of the Ticket Lock is stated as a global parallel theorem. An application of our tactic `method_anno_ultimate` generates six named subgoals. The latter five are side-condition checks, which are easily discharged by `fastforce`, with appropriate lemmas supplied. The main subgoal, presented as the following lemma, concerns the three key steps: *enqueue*,[5] *spin*, and *dequeue*.

```
rely: tktlock_contract i   guar: for_others tktlock_contract i
 inv:  tktlock_inv          anno_code:
     {| ´myticket i < ´now_serving |}
   BasicAnno ((´myticket i ←  ´next_ticket) ○>
              (´next_ticket ←  ´next_ticket + 1)) .;
     {| ´now_serving ≤  ´myticket i |}
   NoAnno (WHILE ´now_serving ≠  ´myticket i DO SKIP OD) .;
     {| ´now_serving =  ´myticket i |} }
   NoAnno ( ´now_serving :=  ´now_serving + 1)
     {| ´myticket i <  ´now_serving |}
```

This RG sentence on an annotated command reduces to three subgoals with an application of `method_anno_ultimate`. These three subgoals correspond to the three instructions in the lemma; each is a RG sentence on a non-annotated command, with pre- and postconditions taken from the appropriate annotations.

On each of these subgoals, our tactics `method_basic` and `method_spinloop` generate named cases, which we easily discharge after identifying and establishing the needed lemmas (possibly with the aid of Sledgehammer).

---

[5] Note that in the *enqueue* step, a left-arrow denotes a function that updates the field of a record, and ○> denotes forward function composition (see Sect. 2).

7   Circular Buffer Lock

Under the Ticket Lock, every queuing thread spins on the same 'now-serving' variable. On cache-coherent machines, this creates extra cache-updating traffic and hinders the hardware performance. This problem can be mitigated using a queue lock where every queuing thread spins on a different memory-location. In this section, we specify a Circular Buffer Lock, which is a more involved implementation of the Abstract Queue Lock, inspired by other array-based locks [2, 8].

First, we define the types `thread_id` and `index` to be synonyms of the natural numbers. We also define a new type:

`datatype flag_status = Pending | Granted` .

The Circular Buffer Lock assumes a fixed number of threads, which we define as a constant `NumThreads`. This constant is assumed positive, which we enforce using a **locale** in Isabelle/HOL. Based on this constant, we allocate an array of size `ArraySize`, which is `NumThreads + 1`.

The state of our Circular Buffer Lock is modelled by the record `cblock_state`, which consists of the following fields:

- `myindex :: thread_id ⇒ index`– a function that maps each thread to an array-index (where the array is modelled by `flag_mapping` below).
- `flag_mapping :: index ⇒ flag_status`– an array of size `ArraySize` that stores values of type `flag_status`.
- `tail :: index`– an index representing the tail of the queue, which is used when a thread joins the queue.
- `aux_head :: index`– an auxiliary variable that stores the index used by the thread at the head of the queue; the head of the queue spins on the flag `flag_mapping aux_head`.
- `aux_queue :: thread_id list`– the auxiliary queue of threads.
- `aux_mid_release :: thread_id option`– an auxiliary variable that signals if a thread has executed the first instruction of `release`, but not the second.

We initialise the array of flags with `Granted` in the zeroth entry and `Pending` in all other entries. The indices `tail` and `aux_head` are initialised to 0. The queue is initially empty, and no thread is in the middle of `release`. (The definition of the initial state can be found in our source files [7].)

A typical state is illustrated by Fig. 1. There are two threads, with Thread 1 preceding Thread 0 in the auxiliary queue. The index held by Thread 1 is `myindex 1 = 0`. As the zeroth entry of the array of flags is `Granted`, Thread 1 holds the lock. The index held by Thread 0 is `myindex 0 = 1`. Thread 0 thus spins on the flag with index 1, and waits for it to become `Granted`.

Similar to the previous queue locks, the `acquire` procedure of our Circular Buffer Lock consists of two conceptual steps. (1) To join the queue, Thread

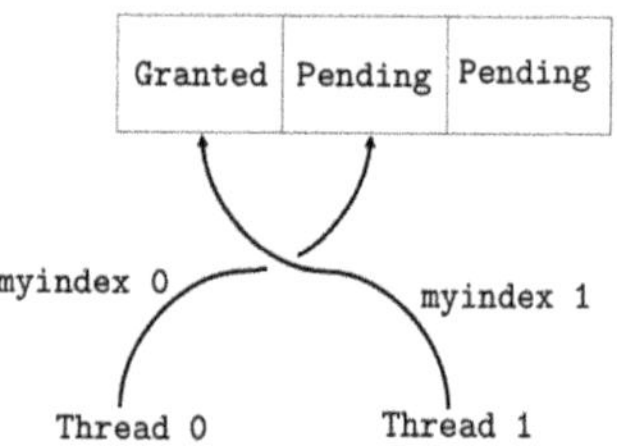

Fig. 1. Example

i stores the global index `tail` locally as `myindex i`, and atomically increments `tail` modulo the array size. (2) Thread i then spins on its flag, which is the entry in the array at index `myindex i`. When this flag changes from `Pending` to `Granted`, the thread has reached the head of the queue.

```
acquire ≡ Basic ((myindex[i] ← tail) o>
                 (tail ← (tail + 1) mod ArraySize)) ;
          WHILE flag_mapping (myindex i) = Pending DO SKIP OD
```

When Thread i releases the lock, it sets its flag to `Pending`. Then it sets the flag of the next thread to `Granted`, which corresponds to 'next' entry in the array, modulo the array size.

```
release ≡ flag_mapping[myindex i] := Pending ;
          flag_mapping[(myindex i + 1) mod ArraySize] := Granted
```

Auxiliary Variables. The `release` procedure consists of the single conceptual step of exiting the queue, but is implemented here as two separate instructions. Hence, the auxiliary variable `aux_mid_release` indicates when a thread is between the two lines of `release`, and allows us to express the assertion there.

The other two auxiliary variables, `aux_head` (the *head-index*) and `aux_queue`, store information that can in principle be inferred from the concrete variables (i.e. the non-auxiliary variables). However, explicitly recording this information as auxiliary variables greatly simplifies the verification process.

In the program, these auxiliary variables need to be updated atomically with the relevant instructions. Below is the code of `release` with the auxiliary variables included. (Auxiliary variables are added to `acquire` in a similar way.)

```
release' ≡
  Basic ((flag_mapping[myindex i] ← Pending) o>
         (aux_mid_release ← Some i)) ;
  Basic ((flag_mapping[((myindex i + 1) mod ArraySize)] ← Granted) o>
         (aux_queue ← tl aux_queue) o>
         (aux_head ← (aux_head + 1) mod ArraySize) o>
         (aux_mid_release ← None))
```

7.1   Invariant

The invariant of the Circular Buffer Lock is stated as separate parts below, all of which are of type `cblock_state set`. The first definition `invar_flag` relates `flag_mapping` with the head-index `aux_head`, and consists of two clauses. (1) At every index that is not the head-index, the flag must be `Pending`. (2) As for the head-index itself, there are two possibilities. When the thread at the head of the queue invoked `release` but has only executed its first instruction, `aux_mid_release` becomes set to `Some i`; in this case, the flag at the head-index is set to `Pending`, but the thread remains in the queue. In all other cases, `aux_mid_release` = `None`, and the flag at the head-index is always `Granted`.

definition `invar_flag` ≡ ⦃ (∀ i ≠ ´aux_head. ´flag_mapping i = Pending)
 ∧ (´flag_mapping ´aux_head = Pending ⟷ ´aux_mid_release ≠ None) ⦄

The next clause `invar_queue` describes the relationship between the auxiliary queue and the other variables, including the set of 'used indices', whose definition can be found in our source files [7]. The clause involving `map` further implies a number of properties, such as the distinctness of `aux_queue` (which mirrors the invariant of the Abstract Queue Lock), and the injectivity of `myindex` (i.e. each queuing thread has a unique index).

definition `invar_queue` ≡ ⦃ (∀ i. i ∈ set ´aux_queue ⟶ i < NumThreads)
 ∧ map ´myindex ´aux_queue = ´used_indices ⦄

The overall invariant is the conjunction of the invariant-clauses above, with three additional simple inequalities concerning `tail`, `aux_head`, and `NumThreads`, which are omitted here and can be found in our source files [7].

7.2   Contract

The contract of the Circular Buffer Lock is devised along the observations: (1) local variables do not change; (2) global variables may change; and (3) auxiliary variables change similarly as in the Abstract Queue Lock.

The first two areas are covered by `contract_raw`, quoted below. The only local variable `myindex` i does not change. The global variable `tail` may change, but is not included in the contract, as changes to `tail` are not restricted. However, the other global variable `flag_mapping` is allowed to change only in specific ways. As `flag_mapping` stores information about the head of the conceptual queue, its allowed changes naturally relate to the *head stays the head* property. Under the Circular Buffer Lock, Thread i is at the head of the queue when `flag_mapping (myindex i) = Granted`. Meanwhile, note that `myindex` i can become outdated if Thread i is not in the queue. Hence, we need the premise i ∈ set °aux_queue before the *head stays the head* statement in the final clause of `contract_raw`.

definition `contract_raw` :: `thread_id` ⇒ `cblock_state rel` **where**
  contract_raw i ≡ ⦃ °myindex i = ªmyindex i
   ∧ (i ∈ set °aux_queue ⟶ °flag_mapping (°myindex i) = Granted
      ⟶ ªflag_mapping (ªmyindex i) = Granted) ⦄

For the auxiliary variable `aux_queue` we require the same two clauses as in the contract of the Abstract Queue Lock. As for `aux_mid_release`, only the head of the queue can invoke `release` and hence modify `aux_mid_release`. Therefore, the second clause of `contract_aux` has the extra equality in the consequent.

definition `contract_aux` :: `thread_id` ⇒ `cblock_state rel` **where**

```
contract_aux i ≡ {| (i ∈ set ᵒaux_queue ⟷ i ∈ set ᵃaux_queue)
   ∧ (at_head i ᵒaux_queue ⟶
       at_head i ᵃaux_queue ∧ ᵒaux_mid_release = ᵃaux_mid_release) |}
```

7.3 RG Theorems

Similar to Sect. 6.3, the overall theorem is a global parallel RG sentence, where each thread runs an infinite loop of `acquire` followed by `release`. Our tactic reduces it to a number of side-condition checks and the following subgoal.

```
rely: cblock_contract i    guar: for_others cblock_contract i
 inv:  cblock_invar i        anno_code:
     {| i ∉ set ´aux_queue |}
   BasicAnno (acq_line1 i) .;
     {| i ∈ set ´aux_queue |}
   NoAnno (WHILE ´flag_mapping (´myindex i) = Pending DO SKIP OD) .;
     {| at_head i ´aux_queue ∧ ´aux_mid_release = None |}
   BasicAnno (rel_line1 i) .;
     {| at_head i ´aux_queue ∧ ´aux_mid_release = Some i |}
   BasicAnno (rel_line2 i)
     {| i ∉ set ´aux_queue |}
```

This lemma is reduced to four RG sentences by `method_anno_ultimate`, with each subgoal corresponding to each of the four instructions. For each of these subgoals, we then apply the suitable tactic to generate a proof skeleton, from which we identify any required lemma, patch any missing piece in the specification, and finally prove the overall theorem.

8 Conclusion

We have presented an extension of the rely-guarantee library in Isabelle/HOL, with the source files freely available [7]. By verifying both high-level specifications (Sect. 5) and realistic code (Sects. 6 and 7) we have illustrated its usability. This extension includes support for RG to be written in familiar syntactic forms, and specifies a global parallel composition operator with global specification components. Commands of the language can be annotated with assertions, which we use to build up a structured representation of commands with pre- and postconditions and intermediate states. Additionally, a common invariant can be separately reasoned about using this framework, instead of repeating this in the four specification components. Novel proof tactics improve readability of proofs, and better assist with specification development and automated theorem-proving.

We have applied the extended RG library to verify a collection of lock algorithms, including an Abstract Queue Lock, a Ticket Lock and a Circular Buffer Lock. In each case, we have been able to reason directly with individual lines of code, using the assertion-annotations and the improved basic syntax structure.

We have shown that all three algorithms maintained their correctness properties when operated under the scenarios outlined by their specification components.

Previously, we have verified an implementation of a CLH lock [5] using some rudimentary proof assistance presented in this paper. For future work, we plan to apply our extended RG library systematically to more case-studies, such as the MCS lock and the networking buffer used in the OpenBSD operating system. We also plan to further improve the library, such as adding support for weak-memory analysis or liveness-property specification.

Acknowledgments. This work was funded by the Department of Defence, and administered through the Advanced Strategic Capabilities Accelerator.

References

1. Amani, S., Andronick, J., Bortin, M., Lewis, C., Rizkallah, C., Tuong, J.: Complx: a verification framework for concurrent imperative programs. In: Certified Programs and Proofs. pp. 138–150 (2017). https://doi.org/10.1145/3018610.3018627
2. Anderson, T.E.: The performance of spin lock alternatives for shared-memory multiprocessors. IEEE Trans. Parallel Distrib. Syst. **1**(1), 6–15 (1990). https://doi.org/10.1109/71.80120
3. Blanchette, J.C., Bulwahn, L., Nipkow, T.: Automatic proof and disproof in Isabelle/HOL. In: Tinelli, C., Sofronie-Stokkermans, V. (eds.) FroCoS 2011. LNCS (LNAI), vol. 6989, pp. 12–27. Springer, Heidelberg (2011). https://doi.org/10.1007/978-3-642-24364-6_2
4. Coleman, J.W., Jones, C.B.: A structural proof of the soundness of rely/guarantee rules. J. Log. Comput. **17**(4), 807–841 (2007). https://doi.org/10.1093/logcom/exm030
5. Colvin, R.J., Hayes, I.J., Heiner, S., Höfner, P., Meinicke, L., Su, R.C.: Practical rely/guarantee verification of an efficient lock for seL4 on multicore architectures. In: The Practice of Formal Methods: Essays in Honour of Cliff Jones, Part I. pp. 65–87. LNCS 14780 (2024). https://doi.org/10.1007/978-3-031-66676-6_4
6. Colvin, R.J., Hayes, I.J., Meinicke, L.A.: Designing a semantic model for a wide-spectrum language with concurrency. Formal Aspects Comput. **29**(5), 853–875 (2017). https://doi.org/10.1007/s00165-017-0416-4
7. Colvin, R.J., Heiner, S., Höfner, P., Su, R.C.: Rely-guarantee extensions and locks. Archive of Formal Proofs (2025). www.isa-afp.org/entries/RG_Locks.html, Formal proof development
8. Graunke, G., Thakkar, S.: Synchronization algorithms for shared-memory multiprocessors. Computer **23**(6), 60–69 (1990). https://doi.org/10.1109/2.55501
9. Hayes, I.J.: Generalised rely-guarantee concurrency: an algebraic foundation. Formal Aspects Comput. **28**(6), 1057–1078 (2016). https://doi.org/10.1007/s00165-016-0384-0
10. Hayes, I.J., Meinicke, L.A., Evangelou-Oost, N.: Restructuring a concurrent refinement algebra. In: Relational and Algebraic Methods in Computer Science, pp. 135–155 (2024). https://doi.org/10.1007/978-3-031-68279-7_9
11. Herlihy, M., Shavit, N., Luchangco, V., Spear, M.: The Art of Multiprocessor Programming, Morgan Kaufmann. 2 edn (2020)

12. Hesselink, W.H.: Mechanical verification of Lamport's bakery algorithm. Sci. Comput. Program. **78**(9), 1622–1638 (2013). https://doi.org/10.1016/j.scico.2013.03.003
13. Jones, C.B.: Tentative steps toward a development method for interfering programs. ACM Trans. Program. Lang. Syst. **5**(4), 596–619 (1983). https://doi.org/10.1145/69575.69577
14. Kim, J., Sjöberg, V., Gu, R., Shao, Z.: Safety and liveness of MCS lock—layer by layer. In: Chang, B.-Y.E. (ed.) APLAS 2017. LNCS, vol. 10695, pp. 273–297. Springer, Cham (2017). https://doi.org/10.1007/978-3-319-71237-6_14
15. Matichuk, D., Murray, T., Wenzel, M.: Eisbach: a proof method language for Isabelle. J. Autom. Reason. **56**(3), 261–282 (2016). https://doi.org/10.1007/s10817-015-9360-2
16. Nipkow, T., Paulson, L.C., Wenzel, M.: Isabelle/HOL: A Proof Assistant for Higher-Order Logic. Springer (2002)
17. Nipkow, T., Nieto, L.P.: Owicki/Gries in Isabelle/HOL. In: Finance, J.-P. (ed.) FASE 1999. LNCS, vol. 1577, pp. 188–203. Springer, Heidelberg (1999). https://doi.org/10.1007/978-3-540-49020-3_13
18. Nieto, L.P.: The rely-guarantee method in Isabelle/HOL. In: Degano, P. (ed.) ESOP 2003. LNCS, vol. 2618, pp. 348–362. Springer, Heidelberg (2003). https://doi.org/10.1007/3-540-36575-3_24
19. Raynal, M., Taubenfeld, G.: A visit to mutual exclusion in seven dates. Theor. Comput. Sci. **919**, 47–65 (2022). https://doi.org/10.1016/j.tcs.2022.03.030
20. Reinhard, T., Jacobs, B.: Ghost signals: verifying termination of busy waiting. In: Silva, A., Leino, K.R.M. (eds.) CAV 2021. LNCS, vol. 12760, pp. 27–50. Springer, Cham (2021). https://doi.org/10.1007/978-3-030-81688-9_2
21. Sanán, D., Zhao, Y., Hou, Z., Zhang, F., Tiu, A., Liu, Y.: CSimpl: a rely-guarantee-based framework for verifying concurrent programs. In: Legay, A., Margaria, T. (eds.) TACAS 2017. LNCS, vol. 10205, pp. 481–498. Springer, Heidelberg (2017). https://doi.org/10.1007/978-3-662-54577-5_28
22. Sanan, D., Zhao, Y., Lin, S.W., Yang, L.: CSim2: compositional top-down verification of concurrent systems using rely-guarantee. ACM Trans. Program. Lang. Syst. **43**(1) (2021).https://doi.org/10.1145/3436808
23. Schirmer, N.: A sequential imperative programming language syntax, semantics, Hoare logics and verification environment. Archive of Formal Proofs (2008). https://isa-afp.org/entries/Simpl.html, Formal proof development
24. Windsor, M., Dodds, M., Simner, B., Parkinson, M.J.: Starling: lightweight concurrency verification with views. In: Majumdar, R., Kunčak, V. (eds.) CAV 2017. LNCS, vol. 10426, pp. 544–569. Springer, Cham (2017). https://doi.org/10.1007/978-3-319-63387-9_27
25. Zakowski, Y., et al.: Verifying a concurrent garbage collector with a rely-guarantee methodology. J. Autom. Reason. **63**(2), 489–515 (2018). https://doi.org/10.1007/s10817-018-9489-x

Template DBM: A New Weakly Relational Domain for Efficient Memory-Access Validation

Yusen Su[1][✉][iD], Jorge A. Navas[2][iD], and Arie Gurfinkel[1][iD]

[1] Department of Electrical and Computer Engineering, University of Waterloo, Waterloo, Canada
{yusen.su,arie.gurfinkel}@uwaterloo.ca
[2] Certora Inc., Seattle, USA
jorge@certora.com

Abstract. A primary goal of static analysis based on abstract interpretation is to infer invariants to verify programs. Memory safety checks (e.g., proving the absence of out-of-bound accesses) require tracking linear relationships between pointer offsets and object sizes, such as `4*idx + 4 <= sz` for accessing memory. Choosing the right abstract domain is crucial, as each domain captures different kinds of properties. For example, Zones and Octagons limit themselves to unit coefficients and cannot express the invariants required for memory safety. On the other hand, the Polyhedra domain can capture any linear relation but does not scale in real applications. In this paper, as a compromise between expressiveness and efficiency while still covering our target properties, we introduce Template DBM –a new weakly relational numerical domain for expressing Two Variables per Inequality (TVPI) constraints with fixed coefficients. Template DBM supports efficient join, inclusion, and saturation. It strikes the balance of expressiveness and cost between Zones and TVPI. We implemented Template DBM in the CRAB library and evaluated it against Zones and Polyhedra domains for memory safety analysis of `aws-c-common` from AWS and `firedancer` from Solana. Our results show that Template DBM maintains its intended level of precision, scales comparably to Zones, and is significantly more efficient than Polyhedra.

Keywords: Static Analysis · Abstract Interpretation · Abstract Domains · Bounds checking · Numerical Domains

1 Introduction

Numerical program analysis powers static analyzers for verification and code optimization across real-world software systems. Although using a precise relational abstract domain ensures accuracy, scalability emerges as a critical challenge when code size grows. For example, Polyhedra [5] domain achieves great precision by encoding arbitrary linear inequalities to capture highly precise program invariants, but its operations incur worst-case time and space complexity

C. Pit-Claudel and K. Kosaian (Eds.): VSTTE 2025, LNCS 16499, pp. 20–38, 2026.
https://doi.org/10.1007/978-3-032-27340-6_2

```c
struct array_list {
  int size;  // allocated size
  int len;   // used length
  int isz;   // item size
  void *data;
};

int get_at(const struct array_list *l,
      void *val, int idx) {
  if (l->len > idx) {
    int ofs = l->isz * idx;
    void *p = (uint8_t *)l->data + ofs;
    assert(valid_access(p, l->isz));
    assert(valid_access(val, l->isz));
    memcpy(val, p, l->isz);
    return 0;
  }
  return -1;
}

void main(int len, int idx) {
  if (0 <= idx && idx < len) {
    struct array_list l;
    l.len = len;
    l.isz = 4; // 4 bytes
    l.size = l.isz * l.len;
    l.data = malloc(l.size);

    // Assume some code initializes l.data.

    void *item = malloc(sizeof(l.isz));
    int ret = get_at(&l, item, idx);
    assert(ret == 0);
  }
}
```

Fig. 1. An example C program.

exponential in the number of variables, limiting performance. However, when scalability is prioritized, some generality tends to be sacrificed. Existing weakly relational numerical domains [16], such as [14,15,20], make their own sets of restrictions.

The TVPI [20] (Two Variables Per Inequality) domain permits any linear inequalities involving up to two variables. It operates in polynomial time, but its inequality set per variable pair can still grow without bound due to arbitrary coefficients. To bound the number of inequalities by the number of variables, one way is to restrict coefficients to unit values, yielding the Unit Two Variables Per Inequality (UTVPI) domains: Zones [14] and Octagons [15] that offer a compromise between precision and cost.

In many cases, program invariants demand more expressiveness than Zones and Octagons provide, but not necessarily the full generality of TVPI. An example in C is shown in Fig. 1. The program takes an `array list` that manages an array with dynamic size but fixed item size (e.g., 4 bytes). Assuming the list is full, copying an array element through function `get_at` requires computing an intermediate pointer p with offset `idx * isz` before access. Establishing memory safety (e.g., proving the memory safety check `valid_access` at line 12 stays within buffer p) requires that the given domain automatically captures the following invariants[1]:

$$p.\textit{offset} + 4 \leq p.size \ \land \ p.\textit{offset} = 4 * idx \ \land \ p.size = l.size \ \land$$
$$0 \leq idx \ \land \ idx < l.len \ \land \ l.size = 4 * l.len \ \land \ l.isz = 4$$

---

[1] We assume a pointer value with extra information [24]: `offset` is the position of the referred object, `size` is the object size. For brevity, we write $l.\textit{len}$ to mean `l->len` for field access..

Neither Zones nor Octagons, which merely express Unit Two Variables Per Inequality (UTVPI) constraints, can prove the check.

Although the generality of TVPI and Polyhedra is useful, it does not justify the computational expense. In our experience, proving the memory safety in low-level code requires reasoning about arrays that are traversed using a stride or a step. Often the size of the stride is the size of a memory word (4 or 8 bytes), or the size of a specific structure stored in the array (i.e., a specific `item_size`). In most cases, specializing the domain to deal with a few fixed coefficients, that are heuristically identified from program source code, is sufficient. Restricting the space of coefficients opens a new opportunity for designing an efficient domain that matches Zones in scalability while adding the desired precision.

We aim to extend Zones to handle TVPI constraints while leaving the complexity of the representation and operations intact. Specifically, we introduce Template DBM, a new numerical abstract domain to express Two Variables Per Inequality (TVPI) constraints with fixed coefficients. Each domain element retains the form of constraints $ax - by \leq c$, where x and y are program variables, a, b are fixed integer coefficients, and c is a constant. For example, a property constraint like `p.offset = 4 * idx`, originally expressed by two TVPI inequalities, is encoded in UTVPI form as $\pm(p.offset - 4 \cdot idx) \leq 0$, where $4 \cdot idx$ is treated as a ghost variable [4] $4idx$. Therefore, TVPI constraints in UTVPI form, as used by Zones, can capture complex properties like array indexing. We fix the coefficients for representation as a template, so the cost of each operation is inherently bound by the number of variables and the size of the template.

In summary, Template DBM is more precise than Zones but less general than TVPI, since it only supports a subset of TVPI constraints. To validate our contributions, we built Template DBM in CRAB [11] and evaluated it in terms of scalability and precision. The evaluation results show that the performance of Template DBM is comparable to that of Zones and the precision measured by the number of memory safety checks validated is close to that of Polyhedra.

The paper is organized as follows. Section 2 covers necessary definitions and operations of the Zones domain. Section 3 introduces a strategy for encoding TVPI constraints in a *difference bound matrix* and provides algorithms for saturation. Section 4 describes the core operations of Template DBM. Section 5 presents the implementation and experimental evaluation. Finally, Sect. 6 discusses related work.

2   Background

In this section, we discuss the necessary preliminaries for the Zones [14] domain, including key definitions and important operations used in this paper.

Given a set of program variables $\mathcal{V} = \{x, y, z, \ldots\}$ with N variables and a set of integer numbers $\mathbb{Z}$ extended by infinity $+\infty$, Zones supports representing a UTVPI constraint system $\mathcal{U}$ over $\mathcal{V}$ of the form: $\{x - y \leq c \mid x, y \in \mathcal{V} \wedge c \in \mathbb{Z} \cup \{+\infty\}\}$. The common data structure to encode UTVPI constraints is a Difference Bound Matrix (DBM), where rows and columns correspond to variables, and each entry represents an UTVPI constraint. For example, the constraint $x - y \leq 3$ is represented in a matrix m with $m_{xy} = 3$[2]. Typically, DBM adds an auxiliary variable v^0 that always takes the value 0 for $\pm x \leq c$. It follows that the matrix dimensions are $(N+1) \times (N+1)$. For brevity, we suppose the variables are integers[3] and ignore describing constraints with infinite value in the rest of the paper.

We assume readers know the abstract domain operations used for building analysis. A DBM supports join $\sqcup^{DBM}$, meet $\sqcap^{DBM}$, and widening $\triangledown^{DBM}$. It also provides a DBMCLOSURE (saturation) operation to derive all implicit constraints, ensuring that the DBM is *closed*. The idea is to propagate inequalities through a transitive chain: given $x - y \leq a$ and $y - z \leq b$, derive $x - z \leq a + b$. The (full) closure operation runs in cubic time $O(N^3)$. For efficiency, we can derive implicit constraints *incrementally* when a closed DBM adds a few new constraints. INCREMENTALDBMCLOSURE does this by updating the affected entries in quadratic time $O(N^2)$. The full details of the core DBM operators can be found in [14], and the incremental closure algorithm for **Zones** is summarized in [2]. Additionally, we assume that the DBM also includes a transfer function such as $m \cup \{x - y \leq c\}$ to add or tighten a set of constraints only.

3   Template DBMs

In this section, we present a new DBM, tDBM (for *template* DBM), that extends the classical DBM for representing TVPI constraints. For any TVPI constraint $ax - by \leq c$ with non-unit coefficients (i.e., $max\{a, b\} > 1$), tDBM introduces extra dimensions for variables with non-unit factors and storing c at the ax, by entry. For example, tDBM associates a dimension for $4idx$ to capture a constraint like $4 * idx - y \leq 0$. These extra dimensions depend on a predefined coefficient template $\mathcal{T}$. We assume $\mathcal{T} = \{a, b, \ldots\}$ with size $|\mathcal{T}| = K$ and always include 1 in $\mathcal{T}$. As usual, we use v^0 with value 0 for $\pm ax \leq c$.

tDBM falls between the system $\mathcal{U}$ and a TVPI constraint system $\mathcal{I} \stackrel{\text{def}}{=} \{ax - by \leq c \mid x, y \in \mathcal{V} \wedge a, b \in \mathbb{Z}^{\geq 0} \wedge c \in \mathbb{Z}\}$ where a, b are positive coefficients. Specifically, a tDBM represents a constraint system $\mathcal{I}_{\mathcal{T}} \subset \mathcal{I}$ over variables $\mathcal{V}$ and coefficients $\mathcal{T}$ of the form $\{ax - by \leq c \mid x, y \in \mathcal{V} \wedge a, b \in \mathcal{T} \wedge c \in \mathbb{Z}\}$.

Figure 2 shows how a tDBM represents the TVPI constraints necessary to guarantee that the `memcpy` (i.e., the assertion on line 12) access buffer `p` remains within bounds. The given tDBM extends two extra dimensions for expressing relations for $4idx$ and $4l.len$. To improve readability, we decompose the tDBM $\bar{m} := (m, m^+)$ into two submatrices: a classical sub-DBM, m, that covers dimensions for UTVPI constraints $x - y \leq c$, and an extended sub-DBM, m^+, that handles TVPI constraints with fixed non-unit coefficients $ax - by \leq c$.

---

[2] Our DBM notation differs slightly from that of [14]: we use $x - y \leq \bar{m}_{x,y}$ for convenience.

[3] DBMs can also be defined over the rationals; however, in this paper, we focus on the integer case exclusively.

$m:$

$$-idx \leq 0 \qquad -l.len \leq -1$$
$$4 \leq l.isz \leq 4 \qquad idx - l.len \leq -1$$
$$p.size - l.size \leq 0 \qquad l.size - p.size \leq 0$$
$$p.offset - p.size \leq -4 \qquad p.offset - l.size \leq -4$$

$m:$

	v^0	$l.isz$	$l.len$	$l.size$	idx	$p.offset$	$p.size$
v^0	$+\infty$	-4	-1	$+\infty$	0	$+\infty$	$+\infty$
$l.isz$	4	$+\infty$	$+\infty$	$+\infty$	$+\infty$	$+\infty$	$+\infty$
$l.len$	$+\infty$	$+\infty$	$+\infty$	$+\infty$	$+\infty$	$+\infty$	$+\infty$
$l.size$	$+\infty$	$+\infty$	$+\infty$	$+\infty$	$+\infty$	$+\infty$	0
idx	$+\infty$	$+\infty$	-1	$+\infty$	$+\infty$	$+\infty$	$+\infty$
$p.offset$	$+\infty$	$+\infty$	$+\infty$	-4	$+\infty$	$+\infty$	-4
$p.size$	$+\infty$	$+\infty$	$+\infty$	0	$+\infty$	$+\infty$	$+\infty$

$m^+:$

$$p.offset - 4idx \leq 0 \qquad 4idx - p.offset \leq 0$$
$$4l.len - l.size \leq 0 \qquad p.offset - 4l.len \leq -4$$
$$l.size - 4l.len \leq 0$$

$m^+:$

	$p.offset$	$4idx$	$4l.len$	$l.size$
$p.offset$	$+\infty$	0	-4	$+\infty$
$4idx$	0	$+\infty$	$+\infty$	$+\infty$
$4l.len$	$+\infty$	$+\infty$	$+\infty$	0
$l.size$	$+\infty$	$+\infty$	0	$+\infty$

(a)   (b)

Fig. 2. (a) DBM-related constraints and (b) a tDBM $\bar{m}$.

The constraint $p.offset - p.size \leq -4$ (denoted as c) is needed to prove the assertion on line 12 is valid. However, this constraint (and all constraints colored in purple) is implicit and can only be inferred from the constraints colored in green. Resolving c requires inferring $c2 : p.offset - l.size \leq -4$, where $c2$ also needs another constraint $c3 : p.offset - 4l.len \leq -4$ to be implied. Section 3.1 shows how to compute those implicit constraints.

For the rest of the paper, we use $row(ax)$ and $col(ax)$ to refer to the row and column indexes, respectively, in the $\bar{m}$ associated with variable x and coefficient a. To access the item in $\bar{m}$, we use $\bar{m}_{row(ax)col(by)}$ or simply $\bar{m}_{ax,by}$ to refer to the difference bounds for inequality $ax - by \leq \bar{m}_{ax,by}$. For elements represented for UTVPI constraints, we write $\bar{m}_{x,y}$. For elements of other TVPI constraints, we write $\bar{m}_{ax,by}$, $\bar{m}_{ax,y}$ or $\bar{m}_{x,by}$. To access the difference bound for any TVPI constraint l, we denote it as $\bar{m}_l$.

A single TVPI constraint can be represented in a variety of equivalent ways. For example, $2x - y \leq 3$ is equivalent to $4x - 2y \leq 6$, $6x - 3y \leq 9$, etc. To keep as many constraints as possible in tDBM, we normalize each TVPI constraint $ax - by \leq c$ into a *template expressible form* so that its coefficients fit the coefficient template $\mathcal{T}$ (if possible). This is justified by the following inference:

$$\frac{\mathcal{I} \vdash ax - by \leq c \quad d \in \mathbb{Z}^{>1} \quad (d \mid a) \quad (d \mid b)}{\mathcal{I}_\mathcal{T} \vdash a' \cdot x - b' \cdot y \leq c'} \; \text{\scriptsize SCALING}$$
$$a' = a/d \quad a' \in \mathcal{T} \quad b' = b/d \quad b' \in \mathcal{T} \quad c' = \lfloor c/d \rfloor \quad c' \in \mathbb{Z}$$

Algorithm 1. Nelson-driven [18] tDBM saturation.

1: **function** NelsonTvpiSaturation($\bar{m}$)
2:     **for** $i \in \{0, \ldots, \lceil lg(N) \rceil - 1\}$ **do**
3:         **for** $x, y, z \in \mathcal{V}$ **do**
4:             **for** $a, b, d, e \in \mathcal{T}$ **do**
5:                 $c := \bar{m}_{ax,by}, f := \bar{m}_{dy,ez}$
6:                 **if** $a'x - b'z \leq c' = $ ScaledResultant$(ax - by \leq c, dy - ez \leq f)$
                then
7:                     $\bar{m} := \bar{m} \cup \{a'x - b'z \leq c'\}$

The rule scales the coefficients by a common divisor d to produce an equivalent inequality, where the new coefficients a' and b' are elements of $\mathcal{T}$. For example, for $\mathcal{T} = \{1, 2, 3, 4\}$, the rule scales the constraint $8x - 4y \leq 8$ to $2x - y \leq 2$ (divided by 4). In practice, we keep just one equivalent form, as others like $4x - 2y \leq 4$ are ignored. The purpose of this rule is to convert TVPI constraints into the expressible forms before matrix updates.

3.1   Saturation

To achieve a full (closed) representation, we *saturate* tDBM by exhaustively deriving all implicit constraints until a fixpoint is reached. We present a saturation algorithm for tDBM based on Fourier-Motzkin variable elimination. Each implicit inequality is deduced following this rule:

$$\frac{\mathcal{I} \vdash ax - by \leq c \quad \mathcal{I} \vdash dy - ez \leq f \quad g = gcd(b, d) \;\; \lambda_1 = d/g \;\; \lambda_2 = b/g}{\mathcal{I} \vdash (\lambda_1 a) \cdot x - (\lambda_2 e) \cdot z \leq \lambda_1 c + \lambda_2 f} \;\; \text{Resultant}$$

which eliminates variable y and yields a new inequality. For instance, consider the two TVPI constraints $2x - 3y \leq 5$ and $9y - 2z \leq 5$. Eliminating y through the rule yields $6x - 2z \leq 20$. If this constraint cannot fit the coefficient template (e.g., $\mathcal{T} = \{1, 2, 3, 9\}$), we apply Scaling rule to rewrite it as $3x - z \leq 10$.

Algorithm 1 saturates an input tDBM by iteratively applying Resultant to pairs of existing inequalities until the iteration limit $\lceil lg(N) \rceil - 1$ is reached. We cap this bound since by then applying the Resultant guarantees a contradiction witness [18]. The Resultant is extended as ScaledResultant which applies Scaling after to produce an expressible form. The time complexity is $O(K^4 N^3 lg(N))$ when a matrix is dense.

Since the tDBM does not express arbitrary TVPI constraints, the algorithm only introduces implicit inequalities within the available dimensions or tightens the existing ones. A tDBM $\bar{m}$ as *complete* if and only if, for every constraint c over a variable set U that $\bar{m}$ satisfies, the projection of $\bar{m}$ (i.e., restricting constraints) to U still satisfies c.

During the saturation process, however, Algorithm 1 cannot guarantee the result tDBM is complete, since the derived constraints may not be expressible in the tDBM. For example, for $\mathcal{T} = \{1, 2, 3, 4\}$, a tDBM $\bar{m}$ represents $\{2x - 3y \leq$

$6 \wedge y - 4z \leq 8 \wedge 3z - 2w \leq 7\}$. Despite the coefficient template, applying the RESULTANT rule iteratively derives a new set of constraints $\{x - 6z \leq 15, 3y - 8w \leq 52, x - 4w \leq 29\}$ at the fixpoint. However, to derive $x - 4w \leq 29$, tDBM requires representing either $x - 6z \leq 15$ or $3y - 8w \leq 52$. Thus, $\bar{m}$ is not complete.

Choosing the coefficient template $\mathcal{T}$ is crucial for completeness. For instance, if the template contains coefficients that are powers of two, running the Algorithm 1 guarantees that all implicit constraints are derived and representable.

Theorem 1. *Given a tDBM $\bar{m}$, Algorithm 1 computes a complete tDBM $\bar{m}'$ under the TVPI system $\mathcal{I}_\mathcal{T}$ if and only if all implicit constraints are expressible.*

Proof. Since all implicit constraints are expressible, Algorithm 1 strictly follows Lemma 1 in [18]. $\qquad\square$

While Algorithm 1 does not promise full completeness, it is sufficient for our purposes. Consider the example shown in Fig. 2, to derive the marked constraint $p.offset - p.size \leq -4$, below are the constraints derived at each iteration:

1. $p.offset - 4idx \leq 0$ and $idx - l.len \leq -1$ derives $p.offset - 4l.len \leq -4$.
2. $p.offset - 4l.len \leq -4$ and $4l.len - l.size \leq 0$ produces $p.offset - l.size \leq -4$.
3. $p.offset - l.size \leq -4$ and $l.size - p.size \leq 0$ gives $p.offset - p.size \leq -4$.

The RESULTANT rule specializes to the standard DBM closure whenever $b = d$, and this closure is not limited to UTVPI constraints. For example, any pair of constraints such as $2x - 3z \leq 4$ and $3z - y \leq -1$ can also use the DBM closure to derive $2x - y \leq 3$. This gives us the opportunity to reuse that routine and to build a tDBM saturation on top of it. Overall, we iteratively apply RESULTANT by decomposing it into two steps:

1. $(b \neq d)\ ax - by \leq c \wedge dy - ez \leq f \xrightarrow{\text{SCALEDRESULTANT}} a'x - b'z \leq c'$
2. $(b = d)\ ax - by \leq c \wedge dy - ez \leq f \xrightarrow{\text{DBMCLOSURE}} ax - ez \leq c + f$

Step 1 aligns TVPI constraint coefficients to eliminate y. Step 2 reuses the standard DBM closure. Accordingly, Algorithm 2 shows a tDBM version in which TVPIREDUCE handles the first step and DBMCLOSURE operates the second. By Theorem 2, algorithm is equivalent to Algorithm 1.

Theorem 2. *Given a tDBM $\bar{m}$,*

$$\text{NELSONTVPISATURATION}(\bar{m}) \equiv \text{DBMTVPISATURATION}(\bar{m})$$

Proof. For any input tDBM $\bar{m}$, Algorithm 2 repeatedly invokes TVPIREDUCE (with coefficient alignment) and DBMCLOSURE (no alignment). This is identical to applying the RESULTANT rule in Algorithm 1. Even the new derived constraint can be used directly during iteration i, with the guarantee of the loop upper bound $\lceil lg(N) \rceil - 1$, ensuring that all implicit constraints are ultimately captured in the matrix, regardless of the order of steps (earlier or later). $\qquad\square$

Algorithm 2. A DBM closure based saturation for tDBM.

1: **function** TVPIREDUCE($\bar{m}$)
2:    **for** $x, y, z \in \mathcal{V}$ **do**
3:        **for** $a, b, d, e \in \mathcal{T} \wedge b \neq d$ **do**
4:            $c := \bar{m}_{ax,by}, f := \bar{m}_{dy,ez}$
5:            **if** $a'x - b'z \leq c' = \text{SCALEDRESULTANT}(ax - by \leq c, dy - ez \leq f)$ **then**
6:                $\bar{m} := \bar{m} \cup \{a'x - b'z \leq c'\}$
7:
8: **function** DBMTVPISATURATION($\bar{m}$)
9:    **for** $i \in \{0, \ldots, \lceil lg(N) \rceil - 1\}$ **do**
10:        TVPIREDUCE($\bar{m}$)
11:        DBMCLOSURE($\bar{m}$)

As the above example shows, the first implicit constraint $p.\textit{offset} - 4l.\textit{len} \leq -4$ is derived from TVPIREDUCE, and the other two from DBMCLOSURE.

Our purpose is extending DBM to support TVPI constraints using a small coefficient template. Experiments in Sect. 5 show that using three active coefficients suffices, and TVPI constraints with non-unit coefficients remain few compared with UTVPI constraints. Thus, running TVPIREDUCE is cheap, and DBMCLOSURE runs nearly as efficiently when only UTVPI constraints are present.

3.2   Incremental Saturation

Existing abstract domains for DBM apply an incremental closure [2,3,10,17] to restore DBM in closed form after each assignment or constraint strengthening, making this procedure the dominant use. By updating only the affected entries in the DBM, the algorithm runs more efficiently than the full saturation (closure) algorithm. In this section, we present a worklist-based procedure that incrementally applies the RESULTANT rule to propagate new constraints.

Algorithm 3 gives the pseudocode for incremental saturation. It adds the new constraint $ax - by \leq c$ into $\bar{m}$. Once the input constraint is tighter, the algorithm first collects all existing constraints involving y (in positive occurrence) and applies the RESULTANT rule to eliminate it, as shown in the purple box, then repeats for x (orange box). Each elimination step produces new constraints that contain only one of the two variables, x or y; we store them in the worklists W_x and W_y, respectively. We present a graph representation (shown in Fig. 3a) that illustrates and highlights the edges added to each list in their corresponding colors. Next, we reuse those derived constraints to completely eliminate either y or x (green box). As a result, none of the new constraints include y and x. Specifically, we derive constraints between z and w through the transitive chain $\{z, x\}, \{x, y\}, \{y, w\}$ (see the green edge in Fig. 3a).

To illustrate how Algorithm 3 works, given a set of constraints with no implicit ones, represented by a tDBM over the coefficient set $\mathcal{T} = \{1, 4\}$:

$$idx - len \leq -1 \qquad size - 4len \leq 0 \qquad 4len - size \leq 0$$
$$4idx - 4len \leq -4 \qquad 4idx - size \leq -4$$

Algorithm 3. Incremental saturation for tDBM.

1: **function** TVPIINCREMENTALSATURATION($\bar{m}, ax - by \leq c$)
2:     $\bar{m} := \bar{m} \cup \{ax - by \leq c\}$
3:     $W_x := \{\}, W_y := \{\}$
4:     **for** $d, e, w \in \mathcal{T} \times \mathcal{T} \times \mathcal{V}$ **do** $\triangleright$ *successors related to y*
5:         **if** $a'x - e'w \leq c' = \textsc{ScaledResultant}(ax - by \leq c, dy - ew \leq \bar{m}_{dy,ew})$ **then**
6:             $\bar{m} := \bar{m} \cup \{a'x - e'w \leq c'\}$
7:             $W_x := W_x \cup \{a'x - e'w \leq c'\}$
8:     **for** $d, e, z \in \mathcal{T} \times \mathcal{T} \times \mathcal{V}$ **do** $\triangleright$ *predecessors related to x*
9:         **if** $e'z - b'y \leq c' = \textsc{ScaledResultant}(ez - dx \leq \bar{m}_{ez,dx}, ax - by \leq c)$ **then**
10:             $\bar{m} := \bar{m} \cup \{e'z - b'y \leq c'\}$
11:             $W_y := W_y \cup \{e'z - b'y \leq c'\}$
12:     **for** $ez - by \leq c \in W_y$ **do**
13:         **for** $d, g, w \in \mathcal{T} \times \mathcal{T} \times \mathcal{V}$ **do** $\triangleright$ *successors related to y*
14:             **if** $e'z - g'w \leq c' = \textsc{ScaledResultant}(ez - by \leq c, dy - gw \leq \bar{m}_{dy,gw})$ **then**
15:                 $\bar{m} := \bar{m} \cup \{e'z - g'w \leq c'\}$
16:     **for** $ax - ew \leq c \in W_x$ **do**
17:         **for** $d, g, z \in \mathcal{T} \times \mathcal{T} \times \mathcal{V}$ **do** $\triangleright$ *predecessors related to x*
18:             **if** $g'z - e'w \leq c' = \textsc{ScaledResultant}(gz - dx \leq \bar{m}_{gz,dx}, ax - ew \leq c)$ **then**
19:                 $\bar{m} := \bar{m} \cup \{g'z - e'w \leq c'\}$

Suppose we add $ofs - 4idx \leq 0$ and perform incremental saturation. The algorithm finds all inequalities involving idx and ofs: $idx - len \leq -1$, $4idx - 4len \leq -4$, and $4idx - size \leq -4$. Applying the RESULTANT rule to eliminate idx yields $ofs - 4len <= -4$ and $ofs - size \leq -4$. With no existing constraints involving ofs, no further constraints can be derived, and the tDBM is once again closed.

Lemma 1. *Suppose a tDBM $\bar{m}$ is closed under system $\mathcal{I}_\mathcal{T}$, adding a new constraint $l = ax - by \leq c$ by Algorithm 3 yields $\bar{m}'$ which is satisfiable if and only if:*

1. $\bar{m}'_{ax,by} \leq c$
2. $\exists o \in \bar{m}, dx - ew \leq f := \textsc{ScaledResultant}(l, o), \bar{m}'_{dx,ew} \leq f$
3. $\exists o \in \bar{m}, dz - ey \leq f := \textsc{ScaledResultant}(o, l), \bar{m}'_{dz,ey} \leq f$
4. *for any constraint $dz - ew \leq f$ derived through the transitivity chain:* $\{z, x\}, l, \{y, w\}, \bar{m}'_{dz,ew} \leq f$

Theorem 3. *Given a tDBM $\bar{m}$ and a new constraint $ax - by \leq c$, Algorithm 3 computes a complete tDBM $\bar{m}'$ under the TVPI system $\mathcal{I}_\mathcal{T}$ if and only if all implicit constraints are expressible.*

Proof. Since all implicit constraints are expressible, Algorithm 3 strictly follows Lemma 1. $\square$

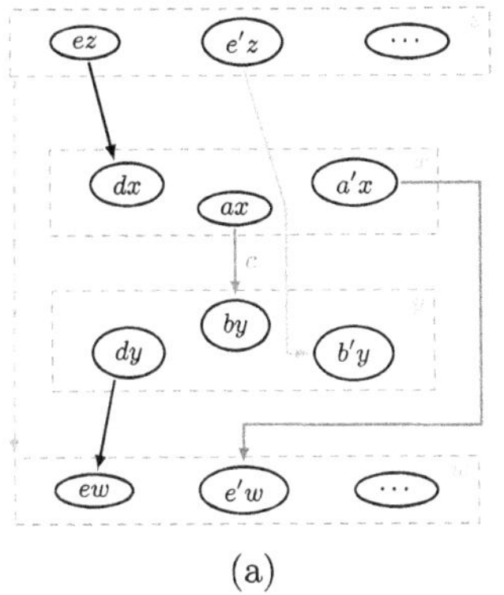

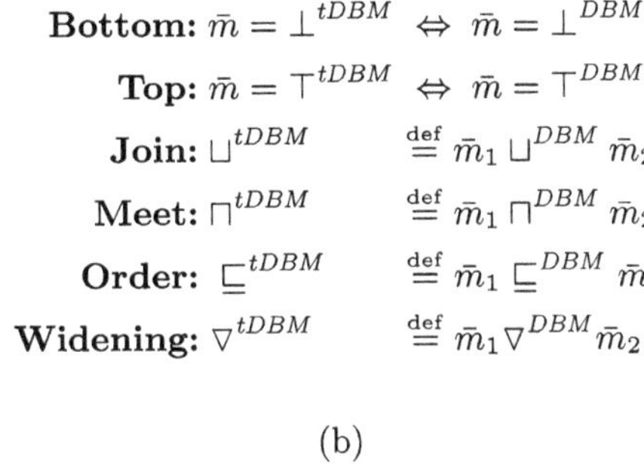

Bottom: $\bar{m} = \perp^{tDBM} \iff \bar{m} = \perp^{DBM}$

Top: $\bar{m} = \top^{tDBM} \iff \bar{m} = \top^{DBM}$

Join: $\sqcup^{tDBM} \overset{\text{def}}{=} \bar{m}_1 \sqcup^{DBM} \bar{m}_2$

Meet: $\sqcap^{tDBM} \overset{\text{def}}{=} \bar{m}_1 \sqcap^{DBM} \bar{m}_2$

Order: $\sqsubseteq^{tDBM} \overset{\text{def}}{=} \bar{m}_1 \sqsubseteq^{DBM} \bar{m}_2$

Widening: $\nabla^{tDBM} \overset{\text{def}}{=} \bar{m}_1 \nabla^{DBM} \bar{m}_2$

(a)   (b)

Fig. 3. (a) Graph view of the tDBM update after adding $ax - by \leq c$ with new edges highlighted and the green dashed edge marking all implicit constraints between z and w; (b) The lattice operations of Template DBM. (Color figure online)

The time complexity is $O(K^4 N^2)$. The correctness of Algorithm 3 is guaranteed by the Lemma 1. Due to the limitation of the coefficient template, running Algorithm 3 guarantees completeness if all implicit constraints are derived and representable in the tDBM. After incremental saturation, contradictions can be detected by identifying negative cycles (Sect. 4).

4 Template DBM Abstract Domain

Template DBM is a new weakly relational domain focused on inferring and checking program properties expressible as TVPI constraints. It is based on tDBM, where each constraint $ax - by \leq c$ corresponds to a specific entry in the matrix.

The concretization function γ maps a tDBM $\bar{m}$ to a set of all possible values assigned for variables that satisfy all potential constraints in $\bar{m}$. Formally:

$$\gamma(\bar{m}) \triangleq \{(s_1, \ldots, s_n) \in \mathbb{Z}^n \mid \forall i, j \in [1..n], a, b \in \mathcal{T}, a \cdot s_i - b \cdot s_j \leq \bar{m}_{av_i bv_j}\}$$

s_i (s_j) represents a value for a variable v_i (v_j).

A tDBM $\bar{m}$ is unsatisfiable (empty) when repeatedly applying the RESULTANT rule yields a contradiction. For example, a tDBM $\bar{m}$ with coefficient template $\mathcal{T} = \{1, 2, 3, 4, 5\}$:

$$2y - x \leq 3 \qquad 5x - 3z \leq -22 \qquad 2z - 5p \leq -2 \qquad 3p - 4y \leq 0$$

It is unsatisfiable because an implicit inequality $3p - 2x \leq 6$ contradicts another implicit one, $2x - 3p \leq -10$, following:

1. applying RESULTANT rule for $3p - 4y \leq 0$ and $2y - x \leq 3$ derives $3p - 2x \leq 6$.
2. from $5x - 3z \leq -22$ and $2z - 5p \leq -2$, RESULTANT derives $2x - 3p \leq -10$.

As Nelson [18] showed that iterating the RESULTANT rule through saturation Algorithm 2 exposes a contradiction. Thus, the unsatisfiable check boils down to inspecting a saturated tDBM $\bar{m}$: $\exists x, y \in \mathcal{V}$, $a, b \in \mathcal{T}$: $\bar{m}_{ax,by} + \bar{m}_{by,ax} < 0$.

A tDBM is bottom (resp. top) if and only if its DBM is bottom (resp. top). For other domain operations, we leverage DBM operations for efficiency. All are defined in Fig. 3b. Each operation performs element-wise matrix updates and runs in quadratic time $O(K^2 N^2)$ at worst. All domain operations are safe approximations, but not the best (except for meet). For example, $\sqcup^{tDBM}$ combines two tDBMs by taking the element-wise maximum of their entries. However, a more precise approximation is obtained by finding the extreme points of the convex hull and reconstructing the TVPI constraints accordingly. Consider a join of two abstract states s_1 and s_2:

$$s1 : -i \leq 0 \wedge i \leq 9 \wedge -c \leq 10 \wedge c \leq -1 \qquad s2 : i = 10 \wedge c = 0$$

The convex hull join computes the result state as $-i \leq 0 \wedge i \leq 10 \wedge -c \leq 10 \wedge c \leq 0 \wedge 10c - i \leq -10 \wedge 10i - c \leq 100$. In contrast, $s1 \sqcup^{tDBM} s2$ as $-i \leq 0 \wedge i \leq 10 \wedge -c \leq 10 \wedge c \leq 0$. While join can be designed using the convex hull algorithm, our design is simpler and takes operations from DBM directly.

The primitive operations during analysis are the addition or removal of variables. For an assignment $x := e$, we define the transfer function (see Algorithm 4) that handles two cases. When e is not a linear expression, we over-approximate its value by its interval $[-e^-, e^+]$; otherwise, we approximate it more precisely by using interval information to iteratively drop variables on e until the remaining constraint follows the TVPI form. We first approximate assignment in UTVPI form, since our tDBM natively represents them. Next, we attempt to convert the assignment to TVPI form. If e involves any unbounded variable, we conservatively approximate its value as $\top$. Finally, we insert each new constraint with incremental saturation to maintain closure. Although more precise approximations exist, this simple approach is effective for analyzing programs such as Fig. 1. As an example, let us consider the assignment `ofs = l->isz * idx` at line 10 with a pre-abstract state:

$$l.isz \leq 4 \ \wedge \ -l.isz \leq -4 \ \wedge \ -idx \leq 0 \ \wedge \ \cdots$$

Although the expression `l->isz * idx` is non-linear, we know from the pre-state that `l->isz` is $l.isz \leq 4 \wedge -l.isz \leq -4$. It is safe to rewrite that expression as `4 * idx` and then invoke the Algorithm 4. The assignment thereby is abstracting as two TVPI constraints, $\pm(ofs - 4idx) \leq 0$, and one UTVPI constraint, $idx - ofs \leq 0$, since idx has a known lower bound. After incremental saturation completed, the resulting state remains closed.

For variable removal, we denote $\exists x.\bar{m}$ for eliminating all constraints on x from the tDBM $\bar{m}$. In practice, this simply means dropping all rows and columns for x (including ghost variables). To preserve precision, saturating $\bar{m}$ is required before existential quantification.

Algorithm 4. Transfer function for assignment.

1: **function** TVPIASSIGN($\bar{m}, [\![x := e]\!]$)
2:     $T := \{\}$
3:     **if** $e = a_1 \cdot x_1 + a_2 \cdot x_2 + \ldots + a_n \cdot x_n + c \wedge \forall i \in [1..n] : a_i \in \mathbb{Z}^{\geq 0}$ **then**
4:         **for** $i \in [1..n]$ **do**
5:             $e_{1i} := \sum_{j \neq i} a_j \cdot x_j + (a_i - 1) \cdot x_i + c$ ▷ *dropping x_i*
6:             $T := T \cup \{y - x_i \leq e_{1i}^{+}; x_i - y \leq e_{1i}^{-}\}$
7:             **if** $a_i \in \mathcal{T}$ **then**
8:                 $e_{ai} := \sum_{j \neq i} a_j \cdot x_j + c$ ▷ *dropping $a_i \cdot x_i$*
9:                 $T := T \cup \{y - a_i x_i \leq e_{ai}^{+}; a_i x_i - y \leq e_{ai}^{-}\}$
10:     **else**
11:         $T := T \cup \{x \leq e^{+}, -x \leq -e^{-}\}$
12:     **for** $t \in T$ **do**
13:         $\bar{m} := $ TVPIINCREMENTALSATURATION($\bar{m}, t$)

---

5   Implementation and Experimental Evaluation

We have implemented Template DBM[4] in the CRAB library [11]. We reuse the implementation from [10] as the underlying DBM which is tailored to make use of a direct graph $\bar{m} := \langle V, E \rangle$. Nodes V correspond to the combination of variables and coefficients $V \times \mathcal{T}$ and each constraint $ax - by \leq c$ is represented as a directed edge $ax \xrightarrow{c} by$. The graph representation avoids the $O(K^2 N^2)$ space of a matrix, since inferred constraints are often quite sparse during analysis [9], especially after widening in loop-invariant computation [21]. Besides, the graph representation can efficiently perform the domain operations. For example, the join can be implemented by merging two graphs and taking the maximum weight for each edge. The inclusion check $\bar{m}_1 \sqsubseteq^{tDBM} \bar{m}_2$ can also be done by checking if all edges in $\bar{m}_2$ can be entailed by edges in $\bar{m}_1$, which can be done in linear time w.r.t the number of edges (inequalities) $|E|$. The implementation for the remaining domain operations follows algorithms discussed in Sect. 4.

For efficiency, we implement incremental saturation instead of full saturation (Algorithm 2) for analysis. It performs local updates on each new assignment or assumption for low amortized cost. Our implementation of Algorithm 3 is based on DBM incremental closure. This special version splits into two phases: first, it runs Algorithm 3 where the RESULTANT rule only applies to cases requiring coefficient alignment; then it invokes INCREMENTALDBMCLOSURE with previously derived constraints to finish saturation. While this version misses constraints since implied constraints from phase two can be used at once, later experiments show that this version preserves good precision and performance.

In the paper, we demonstrate how Template DBM infers constraints to check for buffer overflows in Fig. 1. This example is from a case study in [23], where an abstract interpreter preprocesses the program to prove and remove memory safety checks before a bounded model checker completes verification. These

---

[4] Available at https://github.com/LinerSu/crab/tree/tvpi_dbm.

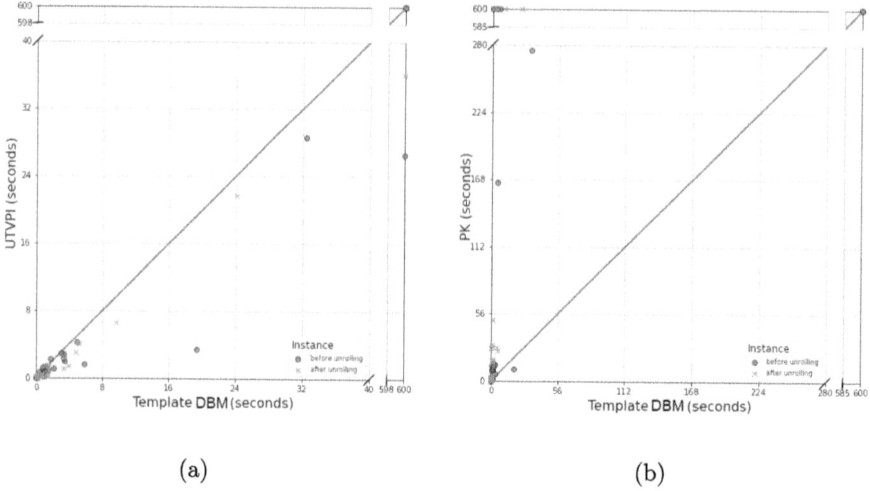

Fig. 4. (a) Zones vs. Template DBM and (b) Polyhedra (PK) vs. Template DBM.

checks as assertions guard each memory access, and the interpreter proves them both before and after loop unrolling. We reuse this study to evaluate Template DBM performance and precision in proving memory safety, while the details of how the interpreter works are outside the scope here. We also omit discussion on interpreter effectiveness, as it has already been discussed in [23].

The benchmark suites originate from two open-source production codebases: aws-c-sdk and firedancer, with a total of 139 benchmarks[5]. Note that benchmarks drawn from aws-c-sdk include the aws-c-common component. These suites cover programs from simple arithmetic computations to complex data structure manipulations. The benchmarks also include loops to evaluate domain operation performance and precision in proving assertions before and after loop unrolling. The experiment here measures how the interpreter using different numerical domains performs as the program size varies.

We compare Template DBM with the Zones (UTVPI) and the Polyhedra (linear inequality) domains. Because Template DBM and Zones use the same DBM implementation, Zones serves as the baseline for precision and performance comparison. We choose Polyhedra instead of the original TVPI [20] because our experimental results (as shown later) indicate that Template DBM achieves nearly the same precision as Polyhedra on most benchmarks. Besides, the TVPI implementation[6] is unmaintained. Having a direct side-by-side evaluation is challenging. For Polyhedra, we use the implementation from the ELINA library [22].

For consistency, we choose the same configurations for running all domains. Template DBM employs a predefined coefficient template $\{1, 2, 3, 4, 5, 8, 10, 16, 24, 32, 40\}$ with 11 heuristic numbers. Each task is given a timeout of 600 seconds.

---

[5] Available at https://github.com/LinerSu/TVPI-Domain-Benchmarks.
[6] The original implementation is at https://github.com/axel-simon/tvpi.

Table 1. Precision across Zones, Template DBM (tDBM), and Polyhedra (PK).

suite	category	Before loop unroll				After loop unroll			
		Total	Zones	tDBM	PK	Total	Zones	tDBM	PK
aws-c-sdk	array_list	24	75%	83%	83%	62	61%	65%	65%
	hash_table	498	83%	85%	85%	2171	54%	58%	58%
	others	1689	67%	67%	67%	2853	56%	59%	59%
firedancer	tango	33	36%	85%	100%	151	17%	85%	100%
	util	106	62%	62%	62%	195	75%	75%	87%
	others	270	24%	24%	11%	305	95%	95%	86%
	total	2620	65%	66%	65%	5737	57%	62%	62%

All experimental results are collected from a machine with an Intel Xeon E5-2680 @2.50GHz, with 256 GB RAM. The artifact and results are available at https://doi.org/10.5281/zenodo.16075045.

All performance results for analyzing each program before and after loop unrolling are shown in Fig. 4. Zones timed out on 5 before unrolling, and on 2 after. Template DBM has 1 more pre-unrolling timeout case than Zones. Polyhedra timed out 8 more times than Zones before unrolling and 1 more after. As shown in Fig. 4a, Template DBM runs slower but remains within a similar range to Zones after excluding timeouts. Before loop unrolling, Zones averages 0.2s (SD = 0.6) and Template DBM 0.4s (SD = 1.9); after loop unrolling, Zones takes 0.1s (SD = 0.5) and Template DBM 0.2s (SD = 0.7). We achieve similar running times because it extends dimensions to support TVPI constraints. Since not all variables require extra dimensions, the size of Template DBM remains comparable to Zones in most cases. However, as the graph shows one additional timeout and one major slowdown (i.e., the 19 seconds to complete), we diagnosed these and conclude that heavily dimensioned matrices harm operation speed. This limitation can be addressed in future work by implementing a more efficient join algorithm and involving a geometric approach to remove redundant constraints, such as the *filter* operation introduced from the original TVPI work [20]. In Fig. 4b, Polyhedra does not scale well, with 2.5s (SD = 15.0) average analysis time before unrolling and 2.2s (SD = 7.4) after unrolling. Overall, Template DBM has performance comparable to Zones and is faster than Polyhedra.

Precision is evaluated in terms of how many assertions are successfully proved in each domain. The compared results before and after loop unrolling are shown in Table 1. We keep assertions proved before loop unrolling instead of discharging and prevent reproving them by adding assumptions. This approach explains why the total assertions grow dramatically after unrolling.

In the table, regardless of loop unrolling stage, the number of assertions proved by Template DBM lies between Zones and Polyhedra. We are more precise than Zones because proving assertions requires TVPI constraints, which Zones cannot express. For instance, in array_list, hash_table, and tango categories, most assertion checks require constraints like $offset * 4 - size \leq 0$ with *offset* as pointer offset and *size* as object size, thus driving significantly different assertion rates across domains. Compared to the "others" category from `aws-c-sdk`, where almost all domains prove the same number of assertions since most checks only require UTVPI constraints to prove. An important observation is that analyzing each benchmark uses fewer than three coefficients from the template. Consequently, the number of non-unit coefficient TVPI constraints grows sparsely yet remains sufficient to verify most assertions.

On the other hand, Template DBM and Polyhedra solve assertions at similar rates across most benchmarks. There are 8 benchmarks where Polyhedra solves extra 9 assertions before and 59 after unrolling. Among these 8 cases, Polyhedra covers more general linear inequalities, such as $x + y + z \leq 10$, that neither Zones nor Template DBM support. Template DBM also fails to prove some assertions due to its limited support for the assignment transfer function. The implementation only handles the form $x := e$ and not scaled assignments such as $24 * x := 24 * e$, though it can be notably improved. However, these assertions represent only a small fraction of all benchmarks and assertions.

In the "others" category from `firedancer`, Polyhedra proves fewer assertions than either Zones or Template DBM. It fails on 79 assertions on 4 cases before loop unrolling and 52 across 4 cases after unrolling. ELINA library logs report coefficient-overflow and vector-product exceptions[7] during these analyses, which cause imprecision. To isolate the ELINA flaw, we use the APRON [13] and PPL [1] Polyhedra as back-ends to verify these cases; either they got the same assertion rate as Template DBM or timed out. We therefore conclude that Polyhedra can, in theory, prove these assertions but, as Table 1 shows, it fails due to limitations in the ELINA implementation.

Overall, our experiment demonstrates that Template DBM offers greater scalability than Polyhedra while providing higher precision than Zones.

6   Related Work

We have already seen some abstract domains close to our work in Sect. 1. This section explores their deeper connections and examines alternative approaches.

The TVPI domain, originally from [20], represents arbitrary inequalities of the form $ax + by \leq c$ with $a, b, c \in \mathbb{Q}$. Our work restricts this to $ax - by \leq c$ where $a, b \in \mathcal{T}$ (a predefined coefficient template) and $c \in \mathbb{Z}$, matching the DBM structure for difference bounds. One way to extend our tDBM is to introduce dimensions ax^+ and ax^- (where $ax^+ = -ax^-$), as in the Octagons domain, to represent more general TVPI constraints $\pm ax \pm by \leq c$. However, this dimensional increase may cause a blow-up and thus degrade performance.

Our work instead prioritizes scalability, which relies on the underlying DBM operations. Template DBM performs saturation to expose all implicit constraints, directly applying the standard DBM operations without altering its structure. In

---

[7] Issue report: https://github.com/eth-sri/ELINA/issues/39.

contrast, the original work treats constraints as a geometric polyhedron, leading to very different design choices for domain operations.

Our work aims to limit the form of TVPI constraints by fixing the coefficient template. A similar approach has been applied in other abstract domains. Logahedra [12] is a TVPI-based domain which restricts coefficients to powers of two. The work also introduces a bounded version, which limits the exponent and thus represents a finite set of inequalities. This version preserves cubic time complexity for core operations like completion and join. Unlike Logahedra, our domain allows custom coefficients, offering a more flexible configuration since array strides are not always powers of two[8]. Template Polyhedra [19] domain fixes linear expressions ahead of time by a predefined template and tracks linear inequalities only for those expressions. As a result, each abstract operation runs in polynomial time relative to the number of template expressions. However, the template must be chosen heuristically at each program location, and each post-condition operation invokes a linear programming (LP) solver to compute the tightest bound for each template expression. Our approach requires only one coefficient template to restrict the TVPI form and computes post abstract states efficiently using the incremental saturation algorithm we propose whenever a new assignment or assumption is added.

The Weighted Hexagon [8] domain captures invariants of the form $x \in [-a, b] \wedge x \leq a \cdot y$ where $a, b \in \mathbb{I}^{\geq 0}$ with $\mathbb{I}$ representing reals or rationals. It features at most six edges per pair of variables and provides a transitive closure algorithm in cubic time. However, it is less expressive because $x \leq a \cdot y$ relations are limited to only the maximal and minimal slopes, and the domain cannot represent constraints with constant offsets. For example, $x - 2y \leq -3$ can only be over-approximated as $x \leq 2y$. The Stripes [7] domain expresses linear inequalities of the form $x - a \cdot (y[+z]) \geq b$ with $a, b \in \mathbb{Z}$. It serves only as a subdomain for the symbolic representation of such inequalities and for propagating information back and forth between other subdomains. It is built in CLOUSOT [6] and serves a similar purpose, but with a different trade-off between precision and efficiency, and with different expectations of surrounding domains. For example, Stripes assumes that equalities are maintained by some other domain along it. This makes direct empirical comparison with Template DBM difficult since they are not easily implemented within the same system.

7   Conclusion

We introduce a new weakly numerical abstract domain, Template DBM, representing inequalities of the form $ax - by \leq c$, between pairs of variables x and y, where a and b come from a predefined coefficient template and c is an integer constant. This work shows how to use a DBM to represent domain elements. We provide algorithms for full saturation, incremental saturation, and lattice operations for the domain. In terms of precision and performance, Template DBM

---

[8] In the hash_table category, we capture TVPI constraints requiring a coefficient of 24, which is the allocation size of a C structure without alignment.

lies between the Zones and Polyhedra domains. Our experiments demonstrate that its runtime is comparable to Zones, while the number of assertion checks it solves for memory-safety verification is close to that of Polyhedra.

References

1. Bagnara, R., Hill, P.M., Zaffanella, E.: The parma polyhedra library: toward a complete set of numerical abstractions for the analysis and verification of hardware and software systems. Sci. Comput. Program. **72**(1-2), 3–21 (2008). https://doi.org/10.1016/J.SCICO.2007.08.001, https://doi.org/10.1016/j.scico.2007.08.001
2. Ballou, K., Sherman, E.: Incremental transitive closure for zonal abstract domain. In: Deshmukh, J.V., Havelund, K., Perez, I. (eds.) NASA Formal Methods - 14th International Symposium, NFM 2022, Pasadena, CA, USA, May 24-27, 2022, Proceedings. Lecture Notes in Computer Science, vol. 13260, pp. 800–808. Springer, Cham (2022). https://doi.org/10.1007/978-3-031-06773-0_43
3. Chawdhary, A., Robbins, E., King, A.: Incrementally closing octagons. Formal Methods Syst. Des. **54**(2), 232–277 (2019). https://doi.org/10.1007/S10703-017-0314-7
4. Chevalier, M., Feret, J.: Sharing ghost variables in a collection of abstract domains. In: Beyer, D., Zufferey, D. (eds.) Verification, Model Checking, and Abstract Interpretation - 21st International Conference, VMCAI 2020, New Orleans, LA, USA, January 16-21, 2020, Proceedings. Lecture Notes in Computer Science, vol. 11990, pp. 158–179. Springer, Cham (2020). https://doi.org/10.1007/978-3-030-39322-9_8
5. Cousot, P., Halbwachs, N.: Automatic discovery of linear restraints among variables of a program. In: Aho, A.V., Zilles, S.N., Szymanski, T.G. (eds.) Conference Record of the Fifth Annual ACM Symposium on Principles of Programming Languages, Tucson, Arizona, USA, January 1978, pp. 84–96. ACM Press (1978). https://doi.org/10.1145/512760.512770
6. Fähndrich, M., Logozzo, F.: Static contract checking with abstract interpretation. In: Beckert, B., Marché, C. (eds.) Formal Verification of Object-Oriented Software - International Conference, FoVeOOS 2010, Paris, France, June 28-30, 2010, Revised Selected Papers. Lecture Notes in Computer Science, vol. 6528, pp. 10–30. Springer, Berlin, Heidelberg (2010). https://doi.org/10.1007/978-3-642-18070-5_2
7. Ferrara, P., Logozzo, F., Fähndrich, M.: Safer unsafe code for .net. In: Harris, G.E. (ed.) Proceedings of the 23rd Annual ACM SIGPLAN Conference on Object-Oriented Programming, Systems, Languages, and Applications, OOPSLA 2008, October 19-23, 2008, Nashville, TN, USA. pp. 329–346. ACM (2008). https://doi.org/10.1145/1449764.1449791, https://doi.org/10.1145/1449764.1449791
8. Fulara, J., Durnoga, K., Jakubczyk, K., Schubert, A.: Relational abstract domain of weighted hexagons. Electron. Notes Theor. Comput. Sci. **267**(1), 59–72 (2010). https://doi.org/10.1016/j.entcs.2010.09.006
9. Gange, G., Ma, Z., Navas, J.A., Schachte, P., Søndergaard, H., Stuckey, P.J.: A fresh look at zones and octagons. ACM Trans. Program. Lang. Syst. **43**(3), 11:1–11:51 (2021). https://doi.org/10.1145/3457885
10. Gange, G., Navas, J.A., Schachte, P., Søndergaard, H., Stuckey, P.J.: Exploiting sparsity in difference-bound matrices. In: Rival, X. (ed.) Static Analysis - 23rd International Symposium, SAS 2016, Edinburgh, UK, September 8-10, 2016, Proceedings. Lecture Notes in Computer Science, vol. 9837, pp. 189–211. Springer, Berlin, Heidelberg (2016). https://doi.org/10.1007/978-3-662-53413-7_10

11. Gurfinkel, A., Navas, J.A.: Abstract interpretation of LLVM with a region-based memory model. In: Bloem, R., Dimitrova, R., Fan, C., Sharygina, N. (eds.) Software Verification - 13th International Conference, VSTTE 2021, New Haven, CT, USA, October 18-19, 2021, and 14th International Workshop, NSV 2021, Los Angeles, CA, USA, July 18-19, 2021, Revised Selected Papers. Lecture Notes in Computer Science, vol. 13124, pp. 122–144. Springer, Cham (2021). https://doi.org/10.1007/978-3-030-95561-8_8

12. Howe, J.M., King, A.: Logahedra: A new weakly relational domain. In: Liu, Z., Ravn, A.P. (eds.) Automated Technology for Verification and Analysis, 7th International Symposium, ATVA 2009, Macao, China, October 14-16, 2009. Proceedings. Lecture Notes in Computer Science, vol. 5799, pp. 306–320. Springer, Berlin, Heidelberg (2009). https://doi.org/10.1007/978-3-642-04761-9_23

13. Jeannet, B., Miné, A.: Apron: a library of numerical abstract domains for static analysis. In: Bouajjani, A., Maler, O. (eds.) Computer Aided Verification, 21st International Conference, CAV 2009, Grenoble, France, June 26 - July 2, 2009. Proceedings. Lecture Notes in Computer Science, vol. 5643, pp. 661–667. Springer, Berlin, Heidelberg (2009). https://doi.org/10.1007/978-3-642-02658-4_52

14. Miné, A.: A new numerical abstract domain based on difference-bound matrices. In: Danvy, O., Filinski, A. (eds.) Programs as Data Objects, Second Symposium, PADO 2001, Aarhus, Denmark, May 21-23, 2001, Proceedings. Lecture Notes in Computer Science, vol. 2053, pp. 155–172. Springer, Berlin, Heidelberg (2001). https://doi.org/10.1007/3-540-44978-7_10

15. Miné, A.: The octagon abstract domain. In: Burd, E., Aiken, P., Koschke, R. (eds.) Proceedings of the Eighth Working Conference on Reverse Engineering, WCRE'01, Stuttgart, Germany, October 2-5, 2001, p. 310. IEEE Computer Society (2001). https://doi.org/10.1109/WCRE.2001.957836, https://doi.org/10.1109/WCRE.2001.957836

16. Miné, A.: Weakly Relational Numerical Abstract Domains. (Domaines numériques abstraits faiblement relationnels). Ph.D. thesis, École Polytechnique, Palaiseau, France (2004). https://tel.archives-ouvertes.fr/tel-00136630

17. Miné, A.: The octagon abstract domain. High. Order Symb. Comput. **19**(1), 31–100 (2006). https://doi.org/10.1007/s10990-006-8609-1

18. Nelson, C.G.: An n^{logn} algorithm for the two-variable-per-constraint linear programming satisfiability problem. Stanford University, Stanford, CA, USA, Tech. rep. (1978)

19. Sankaranarayanan, S., Sipma, H.B., Manna, Z.: Scalable analysis of linear systems using mathematical programming. In: Cousot, R. (ed.) Verification, Model Checking, and Abstract Interpretation, 6th International Conference, VMCAI 2005, Paris, France, January 17-19, 2005, Proceedings. Lecture Notes in Computer Science, vol. 3385, pp. 25–41. Springer, Berlin, Heidelberg (2005). https://doi.org/10.1007/978-3-540-30579-8_2

20. Simon, A., King, A., Howe, J.M.: Two variables per linear inequality as an abstract domain. In: Leuschel, M. (ed.) Logic Based Program Synthesis and Tranformation, 12th International Workshop, LOPSTR 2002, Madrid, Spain, September 17-20,2002, Revised Selected Papers. Lecture Notes in Computer Science, vol. 2664, pp. 71–89. Springer, Berlin, Heidelberg (2002). https://doi.org/10.1007/3-540-45013-0_7

21. Singh, G., Püschel, M., Vechev, M.T.: Making numerical program analysis fast. In: Grove, D., Blackburn, S.M. (eds.) Proceedings of the 36th ACM SIGPLAN Conference on Programming Language Design and Implementation, Portland, OR, USA,

June 15-17, 2015, pp. 303–313. ACM (2015). https://doi.org/10.1145/2737924.2738000

22. Singh, G., Püschel, M., Vechev, M.T.: Fast polyhedra abstract domain. In: Castagna, G., Gordon, A.D. (eds.) Proceedings of the 44th ACM SIGPLAN Symposium on Principles of Programming Languages, POPL 2017, Paris, France, January 18-20, 2017. pp. 46–59. ACM (2017). https://doi.org/10.1145/3009837.3009885

23. Su, Y., Navas, J.A., Gurfinkel, A., Garcia-Contreras, I.: Automatic inference of relational object invariants. In: Krishna, S., Sankaranarayanan, S., Trivedi, A. (eds.) Verification, Model Checking, and Abstract Interpretation - 26th International Conference, VMCAI 2025, Denver, CO, USA, January 20-21, 2025, Proceedings, Part I. Lecture Notes in Computer Science, vol. 15529, pp. 214–236. Springer, Cham (2025). https://doi.org/10.1007/978-3-031-82700-6_10

24. Zhou, J., Criswell, J., Hicks, M.: Fat pointers for temporal memory safety of C. Proc. ACM Program. Lang. 7(OOPSLA1), 316–347 (2023). https://doi.org/10.1145/3586038

An Upper Bound on Number
of Trajectories Required for Reachable Set
Computation of Linear Systems

Parasara Sridhar Duggirala$^{(\boxtimes)}$ (iD)

University of North Carolina at Chapel Hill, Chapel Hill, NC, USA
`psd@cs.unc.edu`

Abstract. This paper presents an upper bound on the number of trajectories needed for computing bounded-time reachable set of linear dynamical systems. The main result of the paper is that for a large class of n-dimensional linear time-invariant systems, only a constant number of trajectories are needed. In fact, only one trajectory is needed; independent of the number of dimensions of the system. This is a strict improvement over the previously presented result where $n + 1$ trajectories were required for reachable set computation. The presented algorithm highlights some of the connections between reachability and controllability. We also give the computational complexity of the algorithm to compute reachable set.

Keywords: Linear Dynamical Systems · Reachable Set · Upper Bound Proof · Star Set Representation · Superposition Principle · Controllability Grammian · Eigenvectors

1 Introduction

The safety critical nature of industrial control systems underscores the importance of their safety verification. A wide class of such control systems can be modeled as linear dynamical systems. An often used technique for proving safety properties of such systems is to compute a reachable set—an overapproximation of all the states reached from a given initial set. Algorithms for computing reachable set (and their overapproxmation) using representations such as polytopes [14], zonotopes [1,16], support functions [15,20], and Taylor models [7] are well known in the literature.

While these techniques are scalable for reasonably high dimensional systems (100s of variables), these techniques are *clear-box*, that is, they require complete information of the system model. An alternative set of techniques that sample various trajectories of the system for computing reachable set have been proposed in [10] to overcome the model requirements. In [17], the authors constructed a metric transition system, which is a discrete approximation of the reachable set, from a sample set of simulations. In [8,9], the authors used sensitivity analysis

C. Pit-Claudel and K. Kosaian (Eds.): VSTTE 2025, LNCS 16499, pp. 39–50, 2026.
https://doi.org/10.1007/978-3-032-27340-6_3

and in [11, 13], the authors used discrepancy functions for computing an overapproximation of the reachable sets by *bloating* the sample simulations.

Computing an overapproximation from sample simulations suffers from curse of dimensionality. The number of trajectories might grow exponentially in the number of dimensions and sometimes is also a function of the safety specification provided. One of the techniques [12] leverages the superposition property of trajectories of linear dynamics and uses a new representation called the *generalized star* to compute reachable set. This technique requires at most $n+1$ trajectories for an n-dimensional linear system. Additionally, this technique is a *black-box* technique, i.e., it does not need the description of differential equations, but only requires a set of sample trajectories. This technique has been extended to hybrid systems in [3] and linear systems with inputs in [4].

This paper is a significant improvement over [12] and presents a new upper bound on the number of simulations required for computing reachable set. Specifically, if all the eigenvalues of the linear dynamics are distinct, we show that only one trajectory, that satisfies a specific set of conditions, is sufficient to compute the reachable set. We also show that any trajectory selected at random will satisfy these conditions with probability 1. While it is commonly believed that *testing can only show the presence of bugs, not their absence*, this paper demonstrates that on well structured systems, one trajectory is sufficient for demonstrating absence of bugs.

We would like to highlight that this paper is primarily a theoretical treatment of the subject and hence makes certain assumptions. First, we assume that all the computations over real numbers are performed with infinite precision. While computations with infinite precision are not always practical, such assumptions are often made while performing analysis of algorithms involving linear algebra and matrices. Since the flavor of algorithms presented in this paper are similar in spirit to algorithms encountered in linear algebra, we believe that such an assumption is reasonable. Extending this assumption further, we also assume that all arithmetic operations over reals take constant time.

2   Preliminaries

Systems considered in this paper consist of several variables evolving in the space $\mathbb{R}^n$. The origin of $\mathbb{R}^n$ is denoted as $\mathbf{0}$. The state of the system is denoted as $x \in \mathbb{R}^n$ and vectors are denoted as $v \in \mathbb{R}^n$. If a vector v is referred to as a state, it represents the state obtained by performing $\mathbf{0} + v$. Given two vectors u and v, we denote the inner product of u and v as $u \cdot v$.

Natural numbers are denoted as $\mathbb{N}$. Given a sequence $\sigma = a_1, a_2, \ldots, a_m$, the ith member of the sequence is denoted as $\sigma[i]$. Given $i \leq j$, the contiguous subsequence $a_i, a_{i+1}, \ldots, a_j$ is denoted as $\sigma[i..j]$. Projection of a state (vector) on the first m basis is denoted as $x \downarrow_m$.

Given a set of vectors $V = \{v_1, v_2, \ldots, v_m\}$, the *span* of V is defined as $span(V) \triangleq \{ v \mid \exists \alpha_1, \alpha_2, \ldots, \alpha_m$ such that $\forall 1 \leq i \leq m, \alpha_i \in \mathbb{R}$ and $v = \alpha_1 v_1 + \ldots + \alpha_m v_m\}$. Given two sets $S_1 \subseteq \mathbb{R}^n$ and $S_2 \subseteq \mathbb{R}^n$, the set $S_1 \oplus S_2 \triangleq$

$\{\, x_1 + x_2 \mid x_1 \in S_1 \wedge x_2 \in S_2 \}$ is called the Minkowski sum of sets S_1 and S_2. The dimension of a given set S is the number of linearly independent vectors in the set. Given a matrix $A \in \mathbb{R}^{n \times n}$ and a vector $v \in \mathbb{R}^n$, the r-Krylov subspace of A and v, denoted as $\mathcal{K}_r(A, b) \triangleq span(\{v, Av, A^2 v, \ldots A^{r-1} v\})$.

2.1   Linear Dynamical Systems

A discrete system is one, where, the system execution is given as a sequence of states. This sequence is also called as *trajectory*. Given an execution of discrete linear systems, the next state in the sequence is obtained by applying a linear transformation, given as a matrix, to the current state. Such a system is denoted using Eq. 1.

$$x^+ = Ax \tag{1}$$

where x is the current state and x^+ is the next state.

Trajectories and Reachable Set: The system trajectory starting from an initial set is denoted as a function $\xi : \mathbb{R}^n \times \mathbb{N} \to \mathbb{R}^n$. For an initial state x_0, $\xi(x_0, 0) = x_0$ and for all $i > 0, \xi(x_0, i) = A\xi(x_0, i - 1)$. We often represent this evolution as the sequence $\xi_{x_0} = x_0, Ax_0, A^2 x_0, \ldots$ A k-bounded simulation from initial state x_0 is the sequence $\xi_{x_0}[0..k]$. We often abuse notation and denote k-bounded sequences from x_0 also as ξ_{x_0} and make the bound k explicit in the context. The bound k is also referred as the *length* of the trajectory. Given an initial set Θ, the reachable set of states after k steps, denoted as $Reach(\Theta, k) = \{\, x \mid \exists x_0 \in \Theta \text{ such that } x = \xi(x_0, k)\}$.

2.2   Superposition Principle and Generalized Star Sets

Superposition Principle: Trajectories of linear dynamical systems (both discrete and continuous) satisfy the superposition principle. That is, given state $x \in \mathbb{R}^n$, vectors $v_1, v_2 \in \mathbb{R}^n$, $k \in \mathbb{N}$, and scalars α_1, α_2, Eq. 2 is satisfied.

$$\xi(x + \alpha_1 v_1 + \alpha_2 v_2, k) = \xi(x, k) + \alpha_1(\xi(x + v_1, k) - \xi(x, k))$$
$$+ \alpha_2(\xi(x + v_2, k) - \xi(x, k)). \tag{2}$$

The observation that trajectories of linear dynamical systems satisfies superposition is well understood in the domain of dynamical systems [5]. It was often referred as the *Wronskian* of the dynamical system [18,23]. While the superposition principle for continuous trajectories has been proved (again) in [12], it also holds for trajectories of discrete linear systems described by Eq. 1.

Lemma 1. *The trajectories of a discrete linear system satisfy the superposition principle.*

Generalized Star Representation: In this paper, we represent sets of states as generalized stars. A generalized star is a tuple given as $\langle c, V, P \rangle$ where $c \in \mathbb{R}^n$ is called the center, $V = \{v_1, v_2, \ldots, v_m\}$ $(\forall 1 \leq i \leq m, v_i \in \mathbb{R}^n)$ is the set of basis vectors, and P is a predicate $P : \mathbb{R}^m \to \{\top, \bot\}$ that represents a subset of $\mathbb{R}^m$. The tuple $S \triangleq \langle c, V, P \rangle$ represents the set of states given as

$$[\![S]\!] = \{\, x \mid \exists \alpha_1, \alpha_2, \ldots, \alpha_m \text{ such that } x = c + \Sigma_{i=1}^{m} \alpha_i v_i \wedge P(\alpha_1, \ldots, \alpha_m) = \top \}$$

We abuse notation and use $[\![S]\!]$ and S interchangeably. From the definition, it follows that $[\![S]\!] \subseteq \{c\} \oplus span(V)$. Since the dimension of any set $S \subseteq \mathbb{R}^n$ is at most n, one needs at most n linearly independent elements in the set of basis vectors V to represent a set using the star notation.

Example 1. Given a two-dimensional coordinate system (x, y), a square $\mathcal{R}$ with vertices $(4, 4), (6, 4), (6, 6)$, and $(4, 6)$ can be represented as a star $R \triangleq \langle c, V, P \rangle$ where

1. Center $c = (5, 5)$.
2. Basis vectors $V = \{v_1, v_2\}$ where $v_1 = i$, the unit vectors in x direction and $v_2 = j$, the unit vector in y direction.
3. Predicate $P(\alpha_1, \alpha_2) = \top$ if and only if $|\alpha_1| \leq 1 \wedge |\alpha_2| \leq 1$.

Generalized stars bear some resemblance to zonotopes, however, they can represent more general shapes including nonconvex and unbounded sets. Any semi-algebraic set $\mathcal{C}$ is in fact a generalized star with origin as center and the orthonormal basis vectors as the set of basis vectors V. Notice that the generalized star representation of a set is not unique. By changing the center and changing the set of basis vectors, one can represent the set in many (possibly infinitely many) ways. The change of center for representing star is equivalent to a *translation of origin* of coordinate system. Similarly, one can replace the set of basis vectors V with another set of vectors V' where $span(V) = span(V')$. This change of basis vectors is equivalent to performing a *linear transformation*.

Example 2. The rectangle $\mathcal{R}$ provided in Example 1 can be represented as a star with center at origin $\mathbf{0}$ while maintaining the same basis vectors. Under such representation $\mathcal{R} \triangleq \langle \mathbf{0}, \{i, j\}, P \rangle$ where

$$P(\alpha_1, \alpha_2) = \top \text{ if and only if } (4 \leq \alpha_1 \leq 6) \wedge (4 \leq \alpha_2 \leq 6).$$

Changing the set of basis vectors to $V' = \{i+j, i-j\}$ would change the predicate as $\mathcal{R} \triangleq \langle \mathbf{0}, V', P' \rangle$ where

$$P'(\alpha_1, \alpha_2) = \top \text{ if and only if } (|5 - \alpha_1| + |\alpha_2| \leq 1).$$

2.3 Reachable Set Computation Using Generalized Stars

In [12], the authors present a technique to compute the reachable set of a continuous linear dynamical system of the form $\dot{x} = A(t)x + B(t)$ using

---

Algorithm 1: Algorithm that computes the reachable set for a bounded time using $n + 1$ trajectories.

---

    input : Dynamics: $x^+ = Ax$, Initial Set: $\Theta \triangleq \langle c, V, P \rangle$, steps: k
    output: $Reach(\Theta) = Reach(\Theta, 1), \ldots, Reach(\Theta, k)$
1 **for** *each i from 0 to k* **do**
2 $c' \leftarrow \xi(c, i)$;
3   **for** *each $v_j \in V$* **do**
4 $x'_j \leftarrow \xi(c + v_j, i)$;
5 $v'_j \leftarrow x'_j - c'$;
6 $V' \leftarrow \{v'_1, \ldots, v'_m\}$;
7 $Reach(\Theta, i) \leftarrow \langle c', V', P \rangle$;
8   Append $Reach(\Theta, i)$ to $Reach(\Theta)$;
9 **return** $Reach(\Theta)$;

$n + 1$ simulations. The algorithm leverages both the superposition principle and the star representation. Since superposition principle also applies to discrete linear systems, we adapt the same procedure for reachable set computation (given in Algorithm 1). Given an initial set Θ in a star representation as $\Theta \triangleq \langle c, V, P \rangle$ where $V = \{v_1, \ldots, v_n\}$, the procedure for computing the reachable set at time k by generating simulations starting from the center c and states $c + v_1, c + v_2, \ldots, c + v_n$. The reachable set at time k is a star with a new center and basis vectors while the predicate remains unchanged.

3   Upper Bound on Number of Trajectories For Discrete Linear Systems

In this section, we reduce the number of trajectories required for computing reachable set from $n + 1$ to 1 under some assumptions. We later provide the conditions on the system when the assumptions hold. The primary principle used in reducing the number of trajectories for computing the reachable set is the following: a contiguous subsequence of a trajectory of linear dynamical system is also a trajectory. That is, given a k-bounded time trajectory starting from x_0 as $\xi_{x_0} = x_0, x_1, \ldots, x_k$, a contiguous subsequence $\xi_{x_0}[1..k] = x_1, x_2, \ldots, x_k$ also corresponds to a trajectory ξ' starting at state x_1 and of length $k - 1$. Hence, n suffixes of a given trajectory can be used as the additional n trajectories required for computing the reachable set.

Lemma 2. *Given dynamics $x^+ = Ax$, and an m-time bounded trajectory starting from $x_0 \in \mathbb{R}^n$ as $\xi_{x_0} = x_0, x_1, \ldots, x_m$, then the suffix $\xi_{x_0}[1..m] = \xi' = x_1, x_2, \ldots, x_m$ is also a trajectory starting from initial state x_1.*

3.1   From $n + 1$ Trajectories to 1 (under Some Assumptions)

Without loss of generality, let us assume that the dimension of the initial set $\Theta \triangleq \langle c, V, P \rangle$ is n. From the definition, one can compute a different representation of the set Θ by changing the center from c to $\mathbf{0}$ and the generator set from V to $V' = \{v_1', v_2', \ldots, v_n'\}$ where $span(V') = \mathbb{R}^n$. Hence, instead of generating trajectories from $c, c + v_1, c + v_2, \ldots, c + v_n$, we generate trajectories from $\mathbf{0}, v_1', v_2', \ldots, v_n'$. Since the trajectory from $\mathbf{0}$ is an invariant for $x^+ = Ax$, it suffices to generate trajectories starting from n initial states that are linearly independent.

Assumption 1. Given a matrix A, let us assume that there exists a vector v such that, the n-Krylov Subspace of A and v is $\mathbb{R}^n$. That is $\mathcal{K}_n(A, v) = span(\{v, Av, \ldots, A^{n-1}v\}) = \mathbb{R}^n$. In other words, the vectors $v, Av, \ldots, A^{n-1}v$ are linearly independent.

While it is not necessary that Assumption 1 should always hold, later in this section, we will present a set of conditions where the assumption holds. If a vector satisfying Assumption 1 exists, then it follows from Lemma 2 that suffixes of the trajectory starting from v start from states that are linearly independent from each other. This is formalized in Theorem 1.

Theorem 1. *Consider dynamics $x^+ = Ax$ and there exists a vector v such that Assumption 1 is satisfied. Consider the $(m+n)$-bound trajectory starting from v as $\xi_v = v, Av, A^2v, \ldots, A^{m+n-1}v$, then, the trajectories $\xi_0, \xi_1, \ldots, \xi_{n-1}$ defined as*

$$\xi_i = \xi_v[i..i+m]$$

are all of length m and start from states that are linearly independent.

Proof. As each ξ_i is a continuous subsequence of length m, it follows that $len(\xi_i) = m$. Additionally, since $\xi_i[0] = A^i v$ and vectors $\{v, Av, \ldots, A^{n-1}v\}$ spans the $\mathbb{R}^n$, it follows that the states $\xi_i[0]$ for $i \in \{0, \ldots, n-1\}$ are linearly independent.

Theorem 1 helps us to generate n trajectories starting from vectors that span $\mathbb{R}^n$ from just one trajectory. Notice that the length of the trajectory ξ_v is of length $m+n-1$ instead of m. Incorporating Theorem 1 into Algorithm 1 gives us verification algorithm (given in Algorithm 2) that uses only one trajectory if Assumption 1 is satisfied. We reformulate Assumption 1 and present it as Theorem 2.

Theorem 2. *Given a linear dynamical system $x^+ = Ax$, and initial set $\Theta \triangleq \langle \mathbf{0}, V, P \rangle$, if there exists a vector v such that the matrix $[v\ Av\ A^2v\ \ldots\ A^{n-1}v]$ is full rank, then, one can construct the bounded time reachable set of Θ using just one trajectory. Hence, an upper bound on the number of trajectories required for computing the reachable set for Θ is one.*

Discussion: Notice that the Assumption 1 has been formulated as a rank of a matrix in Theorem 2. Observe that this formulation is very similar to the controllability grammian condition for linear systems.

Algorithm 2: Algorithm that computes the reachable set for discrete linear dynamical system using just one trajectory from vector v that satisfies Assumption 1.

---

    input   : Dynamics: $x^+ = Ax$, Initial Set: $\Theta \triangleq \langle \mathbf{0}, V, P \rangle$,
               Steps: k, Vector that satisfies assumption 1: v
    output: $Reach(\Theta) = Reach(\Theta, 1), \dots, Reach(\Theta, k)$

1 $\xi_v \leftarrow \xi(v, 0), \xi(v, 1), \dots, \xi(v, n + k)$;
2 $V \leftarrow \{\xi_v[0], \xi_v[1], \dots, \xi_v[n - 1]\}$;
3 Represent Θ in basis V as $\Theta \triangleq \langle \mathbf{0}, V, P' \rangle$;
4 **for** *each i from 0 to k* **do**
5     $V' \leftarrow \{\xi_v[i], \xi_v[i + 1], \dots, \xi_v[i + n - 1]\}$;
6     $Reach(\Theta, i) \leftarrow \langle \mathbf{0}, V', P' \rangle$;
7   Append $Reach(\Theta, i)$ to $Reach(\Theta)$;

8 **return** $Reach(\Theta)$;

Example 3. Consider the discrete linear dynamical system $x^+ = \begin{bmatrix} 0 & 1 \\ -1 & 0 \end{bmatrix} x$. For this dynamical system, let us consider computing the reachable set starting from the set $\mathcal{R} \triangleq \langle \mathbf{0}, V', P' \rangle$ with $V' = \{v_1, v_2\}$ where $v_1 = i + j$ and $v_2 = i - j$ and $P(\alpha_1, \alpha_2) = \top$ if and only if $|5 - \alpha_1| + |\alpha_2| \leq 1$. For computing this reachable set according to Algorithm 1, one has to generate two trajectories, the first starting from v_1 and second from v_2 respectively.

Let us generate the trajectory starting from v_1, say $\xi_{v_1} = v_1, Av_1, \dots$. Let us investigate the second element of this sequence, i.e., $\xi_{v_i}[1] = Av_1 = \begin{bmatrix} 1 \\ -1 \end{bmatrix}$.

This shows that the subsequence $\xi_{v_1}[1..\infty]$ of ξ_{v_1} starting from position is a trajectory starting from v_2. Therefore, for computing the reachable set of $\mathcal{R}$, the trajectory starting from v_2 is redundant as it can be computed from a subsequence of trajectory from v_1. Additionally, since v_1 and Av_1 are linearly independent, one can represent any semi-algebraic set in $\mathbb{R}^2$ using these basis vectors. Furthermore, the reachable set of such set can be obtained by computing just one trajectory starting from v_1.

3.2   Sufficient Conditions For Assumption 1

We will now present sufficient conditions for Assumption 1. That is, given a dynamical system $x^+ = Ax$, we discuss the the sufficient conditions such that Assumption 1 holds. We also present a technique to generate an initial state of the trajectory such that the assumption is satisfied. For this purpose, we leverage the controllability grammian form condition presented in Theorem 2 and search for such vectors for various specific instances of A.

Distinct Eigenvalues of A: We first consider the case where the eigenvalues of A are all distinct. To find out a vector v such that the matrix

---

Algorithm 3: Algorithm that generates a vector v that satisfies Assumption 1 when A has real and distinct eigenvalues.

input : Matrix A with real distinct eigenvalues
output: Vector that satisfies assumption 1: v
1 Compute left eigenvectors of A as $w_1^T, w_2^T, \ldots, w_n^T$;
2 Generate vector v such that $\forall 1 \leq i \leq n, w_i^T \cdot v = 1$;
3 **return** v;

$[v \; Av \; A^2 v \; \ldots \; A^{n-1} v]$ has full rank, we use the following controllability grammian condition from [6].

$$rank([v \; Av \; A^2 v \; \ldots \; A^{n-1} v]) = n \Leftrightarrow rank([A - \lambda I \;\; v]) = n$$
$$\text{for all eigenvalues } \lambda \text{ of } A. \tag{3}$$

Equation 3 that $rank([A - \lambda I \;\; v]) = n$ is well known as Popov-Belevitch-Hautus controllability test [19,21]. This is equivalent to the following condition: given any left eigenvector w^T such that $w^T A = \lambda w^T$, then $w^T v \neq 0$ [2]. Hence, v should not be contained in a subspace that is a span of less than n left eigenvectors. If all of the eigenvalues of A are real and distinct, then one can apply Algorithm 3 for computing such a vector v.

Theorem 3. *Given a matrix A, the vector returned by Algorithm 3 is such that for all left eigenvectors w^T of A, $w^T v \neq 0$.*

Proof. Let $w_1^T, w_2^T, \ldots, w_n^T$ be the left eigenvectors of A. Hence, these vectors are linearly independent. Therefore, the matrix $\begin{bmatrix} w_1^T \\ \vdots \\ w_n^T \end{bmatrix}$ is of full rank. It follows that the vector v that satisfies the conditions in line 2 can be obtained by performing $\begin{bmatrix} w_1^T \\ \vdots \\ w_n^T \end{bmatrix}^{-1} \begin{bmatrix} 1 \\ \vdots \\ 1 \end{bmatrix}$. For such a vector, it follows that for all left eigenvectors $w_i^T v \neq 0$.

Consider the set of eigenvectors $E = \{e_1, e_2, \ldots, e_n\}$ of A as described in Algorithm 3. Any strict subset $E' \subset E$ has less than or equal to $n - 1$ vectors and hence the measure of $span(E')$ is zero. Therefore, upon randomly selecting any vector $v \in \mathbb{R}^n$, the probability that v will satisfy Assumption 1 is 1. This is formalized in the Theorem 4.

Theorem 4. *If a matrix A has distinct eigenvalues, then the measure of the vectors that violate Assumption 1 is 0. Hence, any vector chosen at random from $\mathbb{R}^n$ with probability 1 satisfies Assumption 1.*

Complex Eigenvalues: Observe that when the eigenvalues are real, the left eigenvectors are elements in $\mathbb{R}^n$ and not $\mathbb{C}^n$. When the eigenvalues are complex, that is, of the form $\lambda_i \pm j\omega_i$, the corresponding eigenvector is of the form $(e_i \pm jl_i)^T$. For such instances, Algorithm 3 might yield a vector in $\mathbb{C}^n$ and not necessarily in $\mathbb{R}^n$. Hence, for each set of complex eigenvectors of the form $e_i \pm jl_i$, we construct the extended set of left eigenvectors as $\{e_i^T, l_i^T\}$ and use their union instead of the complex counterparts.

3.3   Systems Where Assumptions 1 Does Not Hold

We now present an example of a system with repeated eigenvalues where Assumption 1 is not satisfied by any vector v.

Example 4. Consider a discrete linear system given as $x^+ = \begin{bmatrix} 1 & 0 \\ 0 & 1 \end{bmatrix} x$. For such system, no matter which vector v you start with, $v, Av, A^2v, \dots$ are all linearly dependent (trivially). Similarly, in n-dimensions, if we consider the dynamical system $x^+ = Ax$ where $A = eye(n)$ is the identity matrix, then $\forall v \in \mathbb{R}^n$, $v, Av, A^2v, \dots$ are all linearly dependent.

The authors conjecture that for any matrix A with repeated eigenvalue $\lambda \neq 1$, one can construct similar extended eigenvectors and apply Algorithm 3 for generating the vector v that satisfies Assumption 1.

Remark: Notice that the Assumption 1 is closely related to the notion of controllability grammian. While the relationship between the controllability and reachability for discrete linear systems has been established in [22], to the authors knowledge, this is the first paper that uses a result in controllability to *compute* the reachable set of states for a given initial set.

4   Extension to Continuous Systems

The reachable set computation for continuous linear systems of the form $\dot{x} = Ax$ is similar to the algorithm for the discrete system. Hence, extension of the upper bound result to trajectories of continuous dynamical system closely imitates the discrete counterpart.

The trajectories of continuous linear systems are $\xi : \mathbb{R}^n \times \mathbb{R}_{\geq 0} \to \mathbb{R}^n$ is given as $\xi(x_0, t) = e^{At}x_0$ where $e^{At} = I + At + \frac{A^2 t^2}{2!} + \frac{A^3 t^3}{3!} + \dots$. Given a trajectory ξ, and $0 \leq lb \leq ub$, $\xi[lb..ub]$ denotes the trajectory with the time restricted to the interval $[lb..ub]$. The length of $\xi[lb..ub]$ is $ub - lb$.

Lemma 3. *Given dynamics $\dot{x} = Ax$, a bounded trajectory $\xi_v : [0, T] \to \mathbb{R}^n$ ($T > 0$) such that $\forall t \in [0, T], \xi_v(t) = e^{At}v$, and a value $0 < h < T$ then $\xi' = \xi_v[h..T]$ is also a trajectory of length $T - h$ starting from $\xi_v(h)$.*

Algorithm 4: Algorithm that computes the reachable set for continuous linear dynamical system using just 1 trajectory from vector v that satisfies Assumption 2.

---

input : Dynamics: $\dot{x} = Ax$, Initial Set: $\Theta \triangleq \langle \mathbf{0}, V, P \rangle$,
         time: t, Vector that satisfies assumption 2: v
output: $Reach(\Theta, t)$

1 $\xi_v \leftarrow \xi(v, \cdot)$;
2 $\mathcal{V} \leftarrow \{\xi_v[0], \xi_v[h], \ldots, \xi_v[(n-1)h]\}$;
3 Represent Θ in basis $\mathcal{V}$ as $\Theta \triangleq \langle 0, \mathcal{V}, P' \rangle$;
4 **for** *each i from 1 to n* **do**
5      $v_i' \leftarrow \xi_v[t + (i-1) \cdot h]$;
6 $V' \leftarrow \{v_1', \ldots, v_n'\}$;
7 $Reach(\Theta, t) \leftarrow \langle \mathbf{0}, V', P' \rangle$;
8 **return** $Reach(\Theta, t)$;

Proof. Similar to the proof of Lemma 2, follows trivially from the closed form expression of trajectory.

Assumption 2. Given a matrix A, and a positive real number h, let $A_h = e^{Ah}$. Suppose that there exists a vector v such that the n-Krylov Subspace of A_h and v spans $\mathbb{R}^n$, that is, $\mathcal{K}_n(A_h, v) = span(\{v, A_h v, \ldots, A_h^{n-1} v\}) = \mathbb{R}^n$.

Theorem 5. *Assume that there exists vector v and $h > 0$ such that Assumption 2 is satisfied. Now consider the $T + n \cdot h$ time bound trajectory starting from v as $\xi_v : [0, T + n \cdot h] \to \mathbb{R}^n$ then the trajectories $\xi_0, \xi_1, \ldots, \xi_{n-1}$ defined as*

$$\xi_i = \xi_v[(i \cdot h)..(T + i \cdot h)]$$

are all of length T and start from states that are linearly independent.

Proof. Follows from Assumption 2 and similar to the proof of Theorem 1.

We now present the algorithm that computes the reachable set of Θ at time $t \in [0, T]$ using just one trajectory in Algorithm 4.

Since the left eigenvectors of e^{Ah} are same as the left eigenvectors for matrix A, the Algorithm 3 can be employed to compute a vector v that satisfies Assumption 2.

5   Conclusions

In this paper, we presented an upper bound on the number of trajectories required for computing reachable set of discrete linear dynamical systems. For linear dynamics with distinct eigenvalues, only one simulation suffices to compute the reachable set. While the number of simulations is independent of the number of dimensions, the duration of the simulation in the case of discrete system, is of length at least $n + k$ where k is time bound for verification. This paper also presents interesting connections between the controllability and reachable set computation techniques. One of the important contributions of this paper is that it establishes that one can compute symbolic representation of reachable set from a single trajectory of the system behavior.

As a part of future work, the authors would like to investigate the case of repeated eigenvalues and resolve the conjecture. Additionally, we would like to extend this to hybrid systems and investigate the issues of numerical stability at a greater detail on a prototype implementation. Finally, the authors would like to extend this work to program verification and compute polyhedral over-approximation of reachable set from mere one execution of the program.

References

1. Althoff, M.: An introduction to cora. In: Proceedings of the Workshop on Applied Verification for Continuous and Hybrid Systems (2015)
2. Antsaklis, P.J., Michel, A.N.: A Linear Systems Primer, vol. 1. Birkhäuser Boston (2007)
3. Bak, S., Duggirala, P.S.: Rigorous simulation-based analysis of linear hybrid systems. In: Tools and Algorithms for the Construction and Analysis of Systems, pp. 555–572 (2017)
4. Bak, S., Duggirala, P.S.: Simulation-equivalent reachability of large linear systems with inputs. In: Computer Aided Verification - 29th International Conference, CAV, pp. 401–420 (2017)
5. Bender, C.M., Orszag, S.A.: Advanced Mathematical Methods for Scientists and Engineers I: Asymptotic Methods and Perturbation Theory. Springer, Heidelberg (2013). https://doi.org/10.1007/978-1-4757-3069-2
6. Chen, C.-T.: Linear System Theory and Design. Oxford University Press Inc. (1995)
7. Chen, X., Ábrahám, E., Sankaranarayanan, S.: Flow*: an analyzer for non-linear hybrid systems. In: Computer Aided Verification, pp. 258–263 (2013)
8. Donzé, A.: Breach, a toolbox for verification and parameter synthesis of hybrid systems. In: Touili, T., Cook, B., Jackson, P. (eds.) CAV 2010. LNCS, vol. 6174, pp. 167–170. Springer, Heidelberg (2010). https://doi.org/10.1007/978-3-642-14295-6_17
9. Donzé, A., Maler, O.: Systematic simulation using sensitivity analysis. In: HSCC, pp. 174–189 (2007)
10. Sridhar Duggirala, P.: Dynamic analysis of cyber-physical systems. University of Illinois at Urbana-Champaign (2015)
11. Sridhar Duggirala, P., Mitra, S., Viswanathan, M.: Verification of annotated models from executions. In: Proceedings of the 13th International Conference on Embedded Software (EMSOFT 2013) (2013)
12. Duggirala, P.S., Viswanathan, M.: Parsimonious, simulation based verification of linear systems. In: Chaudhuri, S., Farzan, A. (eds.) CAV 2016. LNCS, vol. 9779, pp. 477–494. Springer, Cham (2016). https://doi.org/10.1007/978-3-319-41528-4_26
13. Fan, C., Mitra, S.: Bounded verification with on-the-fly discrepancy computation. In: 13th International Symposium on Automated Technology for Verification and Analysis (2015)

14. Frehse, G.: Phaver: algorithmic verification of hybrid systems past hytech. Int. J. Softw. Tools Technol. Transfer (STTT) **10**(3) (2008)
15. Frehse, G., et al.: SpaceEx: scalable verification of hybrid systems. In: Gopalakrishnan, G., Qadeer, S. (eds.) CAV 2011. LNCS, vol. 6806, pp. 379–395. Springer, Heidelberg (2011). https://doi.org/10.1007/978-3-642-22110-1_30
16. Girard, A.: Reachability of uncertain linear systems using zonotopes. In: International Workshop on Hybrid Systems: Computation and Control, pp. 291–305 (2005)
17. Girard, A., Pappas, G.J.: Verification using simulation. In: Hespanha, J.P., Tiwari, A. (eds.) HSCC 2006. LNCS, vol. 3927, pp. 272–286. Springer, Heidelberg (2006). https://doi.org/10.1007/11730637_22
18. Hartman, P.: Ordinary differential equations. SIAM (2002)
19. Hautus, M.L.J.: Controllability and observability conditions of linear autonomous systems. In: Proceedings of the Koninklijke Nederlandse Akademie Van Wetenschappen Series a-Mathematical Sciences, vol. 72, no. 5, p. 443 (1969)
20. Le Guernic, C., Girard, A.: Reachability analysis of linear systems using support functions. Nonlinear Anal. Hybrid Syst **4**(2), 250–262 (2010)
21. Popov, V.M.: Invariant description of linear, time-invariant controllable systems. SIAM J. Control **10**(2), 252–264 (1972)
22. Sontag, E.D.: Mathematical Control Theory: Deterministic Finite Dimensional Systems, vol. 6. Springer, Heidelberg (2013)
23. Wolsson, K.: Linear dependence of a function set of m variables with vanishing generalized wronskians. Linear Algebra Appl. **117**, 73–80 (1989)

Verifying the Functional Correctness
of Braun Trees with LiquidHaskell

Felipe de León(✉)[iD], Alberto Pardo[iD], and Marcos Viera[iD]

Instituto de Computación, Universidad de la República, Montevideo, Uruguay
`{felipe.de.leon,pardo,mviera}@fing.edu.uy`

Abstract. LiquidHaskell is an extension to Haskell that enhances its
type system with refinement types, enabling the integration of formal
verification to software development by the introduction of type annotations in the form of logical predicates in data structure and function
definitions. In this paper, we explore the specification and verification
capabilities of LiquidHaskell by focusing on balanced trees, and more
specifically on Braun trees, a data structure used for representing functional arrays. We formalize some properties of balanced trees, concerning
the relationship between their height and number of nodes. On top of
these properties, we verify the invariants of functional and flexible arrays,
resulting in an implementation that encodes most of the pre-conditions
and post-conditions that preserve such invariants.

Keywords: LiquidHaskell · Verification · BraunTrees · Functional
Arrays

1 Introduction

Formal verification has long promised increased software reliability, but its integration into mainstream programming practices remains limited due to complexity, verbosity, and steep learning curves. Since its introduction, LiquidHaskell
(LH) [13] has been advertised as a lightweight approach to integrate formal verification into Haskell, offering a balance between expressiveness, low verbosity,
and practical performance.

The aim of this work is to experiment with the main formalization and verification features of LH, applying them to a non-trivial example. In this sense, we
focus on the formalization of functional arrays by means of their implementation
in terms of Braun trees [2], a class of balanced binary trees with a well-defined
structural property and efficient indexing operations. Due to their regular shape,
Braun trees serve as an excellent benchmark to test the formal verification capabilities of LH. Braun trees are an interesting use case, since they are simple
enough to admit elegant specifications, yet rich enough to expose the limits and
power of current verification tools.

Our development is strongly guided by the work of Nipkow and Sewell [6],
who present a comprehensive formalization of Braun trees in Isabelle/HOL. We

C. Pit-Claudel and K. Kosaian (Eds.): VSTTE 2025, LNCS 16499, pp. 51–70, 2026.
https://doi.org/10.1007/978-3-032-27340-6_4

replicate their verification effort, adapting the invariant definitions and their verification to the realm of LH.

In summary, we make the following contributions: (i) we formalize balanced binary trees in LH and prove some of their logarithmic properties; (ii) we formalize functional and flexible arrays implemented using Braun trees; and (iii) we use Braun trees as a use case to explore recent LH features for theorem proving and refinement type reasoning, comparing them with those of other theorem provers.

The rest of the paper is organized as follows. In Sect. 2 we briefly describe the main features of LH. Then, in Sect. 3, we prove some logarithmic properties that balanced binary trees satisfy. On top of these properties, in Sect. 4, we prove the balance property of Braun trees and verify a series of invariants for operations on functional arrays. In Sect. 4.3 we verify flexible arrays, implemented in terms of Braun trees. Finally, we discuss related work in Sect. 5 and present some conclusions in Sect. 6.

The complete implementation, including all definitions, operations, and mechanized proofs, is available at https://gitlab.fing.edu.uy/felipe.de.leon/brauntrees.

2   LiquidHaskell

LH [3] is an extension to Haskell that enhances its type system with refinement types, enabling programmers to specify and verify correctness properties of their code at compile time, going beyond what standard Haskell types can express. Those properties are given by logical predicates that can be regarded as Haskell Boolean expressions which can be verified by an SMT solver. For example, we can define a safe division operation by declaring a pre-condition that restricts the divisor to be non-zero:

```
{-@ safe_div :: Int -> d : { Int | d != 0 } -> Int @-}
safe_div :: Int -> Int -> Int
safe_div x y = div x y
```

By annotating the non-zero condition in the type of the second argument, we ensure that, when compiled, LH checks that in our code there is no case where `safe_div` is called with zero as divisor. If LH finds such a case, compilation fails and a proper error message is shown. Under the hood this means that the SMT solver found a case where the equation is not satisfied producing an error.

2.1   Promoting Functions

LH does not directly interpret Haskell functions within its refinement logic; functions are treated as black boxes. In order to reason about their behaviour, one can promote them to refinement logic using specific directives provided by LH.

Inline. The `inline` directive allows the promotion of non-recursive functions whose body is composed by other already-promoted functions. It is mostly used to promote simple predicates. An example is the following function that checks for non-zero values:

```
{-@ inline notZero @-}
notZero :: Int -> Bool
notZero x = x != 0
```

Once promoted, we can call these function inside refinements. For example, we can rewrite the signature of `safe_div` as:

```
{-@ safe_div :: Int -> d : { Int | notZero d } -> Int @-}
```

Measure. Functions promoted with the `measure` [12] directive must be structurally recursive on a decreasing argument and accept only a single parameter. In this case LH internally generates a refinement type where the promoted function definition is attached to the data constructor of the type of the parameter. If multiple measures are defined, they are merged into a single constructor.

For instance, we can define a function `allEven`, to check if all the elements of a list of integers are even, and promote it using `measure`:

```
{-@ measure allEven @-}
allEven :: [Int] -> Bool
allEven []       = True
allEven (x:xs) = even x && allEven xs
```

Having this function promoted, we can now use it to define e.g. the domain of lists of even numbers:

```
{-@ lstEvens :: xs : { [Int] | allEven xs } @-}
lstEvens = [2,4,6,8]
```

LH will verify that the list `lstEvens` indeed contains only even numbers.

The `type` directive can be used to define a named refinement type, allowing reusable and more readable specifications. Thus, if we define:

```
{-@ type EvenList = { xs : [Int] | allEven xs } @-}
```

the annotation for `lstEvens` can be simplified to:

```
{-@ lstEvens :: EvenList @-}
```

Reflection. The `reflect` directive comes with slightly fewer limitations than the previous two. When a function is promoted with `reflect`, LH introduces an uninterpreted version of it in the refinement logic and embeds its body for use in logical reasoning. Once reflected, a function can be unfolded in logic formulas, allowing it to participate in more expressive proofs and theorem statements.

Unlike measures, reflected functions can have multiple parameters and can call other reflected functions but their will be require to terminate. Also different from measures, reflected functions do not bind values to constructors, but add constraints to the result of the functions. For this reason, if we try to promote `allEven` using reflection, then LH is unable to check that a given list contains only even numbers unless that is explicitly verified elsewhere.

Reflected functions on their own are less powerful than measures. However, Vazou [10] developed a library of proof combinators, which allow the use of LH as a theorem prover. The library includes the following combinators: `Proof`, an alias for the unit type () indicating we are proving a theorem; `QED`, declares that a proof is ready; (`***`), marks the end of a proof before `QED`; (`===`), equality between expressions in an equational proof; `?`, the "because" operator, used to justify steps in proofs; and `&&&`, an AND operator that allows the combination of subproofs, e.g. when proofs are divided into cases.

For instance, using some of these combinators we can write a proof stating that a list contains only even elements:

```
{-@ lstEvens_prf :: {allEven [2,4,6,8] == True} @-}
lstEvens_prf :: Proof
lstEvens_prf = allEven [2,4,6,8]
             === (even 2 && allEven [4,6,8])
             === (even 4 && allEven [6,8])
             === (even 6 && allEven [8])
             === (even 8 && allEven []) *** QED
```

Every time it is applied to an even number, `even` returns `True`. Since we are using the Boolean `&&` operator, we can eliminate the intermediate `True` values in the proof, allowing us to simplify step by step until we reach the final result. The rest of the combinators will be used later, when we show more complex proofs.

PLE. Proof by Logical Evaluation (PLE) [10,11] is a feature of LH that adds the following steps during type checking: (i) transforms every function into its reflected form; (ii) unfolds the reflected functions; and (iii) repeats until a fixpoint is reached.

When PLE is enabled, the earlier `allEven` example can be automatically verified without having to write the proof for `lstEvens_prf`; i.e., we can either define `lstEvens` as in the measure example or define `lstEvens_prf` just as ().

As we will see later, while PLE is very effective for simple equational reasoning and inductive properties, it cannot always handle complex recursion, higher-order functions, or proofs that require more sophisticated case analysis or user guidance.

3   Balanced Binary Trees

Balanced trees are a very common structure to formalize, as their structural constraints make them a good case study for verification tools. Previous work in LH regarding balanced trees focuses on AVL trees [9] and red-black trees [13]. In this work, we focus on some logarithmic properties that these structures satisfy.

The representation of balanced binary trees in LH starts with the definition of (parameterized) binary trees:

```
data Tree a  = Node a (Tree a) (Tree a) | Nil
```

Following [6], we say that a tree is balanced if the absolute difference between its maximum and minimum height is at most 1.

```
{-@ measure balanced @-}
{-@ balanced :: Tree a -> Bool @-}
balanced Nil              = True
balanced t@(Node _ l r) = balanced l && balanced r &&
                          h t - mh t <= 1
```

Functions `h` and `mh` denote the maximum and minimum heights of the tree, respectively, i.e. the lengths of the longest and shortest paths from the root to a leaf. Since `mh` is always less than or equal to `h`, we encode this invariant in the function's return type. LH is able to prove it automatically. This allows us to directly write `h t - mh t <= 1`, knowing that the value will always be between 0 and 1 (and never negative). We only show the signatures and annotations of `h` and `mh`, their definitions are straightforward.

```
{-@ measure h @-}
{-@ h :: t: Tree a -> i : { Nat | i >= mh t }  @-}
h :: Tree a -> Int

{-@ measure mh @-}
{-@ mh :: t : Tree a -> i : { Nat | i <= h t } @-}
mh :: Tree a -> Int
```

We deliberately promote this function using **measure**, as we want the balance information to be embedded directly in the constructor of the tree. By promoting in such way, we strengthen the type system, allowing us to perform more granular pattern matching and, obtaining more precise information about the structure we are working with. If we had used **reflect** instead, the effectiveness would depend on how far the solver is able to unfold the definitions. In this case, we find that **measure** is more powerful than **reflect** when defining properties over data types.

Although the condition `h t - mh t <= 1` is sufficient to consider a tree balanced, we also explicitly require that the left and right subtrees are balanced. The addition of this extra condition on the subtrees is useful in future proofs to avoid repeatedly establishing that subtrees meet the balance condition.

Finally, we define the **BTree** structure, which consists of those trees that satisfy the definition of **balanced**.

```
{-@ type BTree a = { t: Tree a | balanced t } @-}
```

Every time we specify a tree as a **BTree**, LH automatically enforces the corresponding balance restriction on the structure. For example, if we try to construct a tree with three consecutive nodes on the left, then LH produces a type error, indicating that t does not satisfy the definition of a BTree i.e.: Node 1 (Node 2 (Node 3 Nil Nil)Nil)Nil.

```
{-@ prop_2 :: t : BTree a -> { log2F (nc t + 1) == mh t } @-}
prop_2 t = log2F (nc t + 1) == mh t ?
           ((nc t + 1 >= pow2 (mh t) ? prop_4 t) *** QED)
         &&&
           (nc t + 1 < pow2 (mh t + 1) ? prop_3 t *** QED))
         ? prop_5 (mh t) (nc t + 1) *** QED
```

Fig. 1. Proof of property (2).

3.1 Logarithmic Properties

Once we have established our structure to refer to balanced trees, we want to prove some standard properties about them using LH, in particular those concerning the relationship between the height of a tree and its number of nodes.

$$balanced(t) \Rightarrow h(t) = \lceil \log_2(nc(t) + 1) \rceil \tag{1}$$
$$balanced(t) \Rightarrow mh(t) = \lfloor \log_2(nc(t) + 1) \rfloor \tag{2}$$

Function nc counts the number of nodes of a given tree (we omit its definition because it is straightforward).

To prove these properties, we first define the floor and ceiling of the logarithm, since LH lacks built-in support for logarithmic operations. We compute the floor of the base-2 logarithm of a number n, log2F n, by counting how many times n can be divided by 2 until it reaches 0. The ceiling of the logarithm, log2C n, is then derived from log2F n by incrementing the result by 1 when pow2 (log2F n)== n.

We start with the proof of property (2). Its main ingredients are the following auxiliary properties:

$$balanced(t) \Rightarrow nc(t) + 1 < 2^{mh(t)+1} \tag{3}$$
$$balanced(t) \Rightarrow nc(t) \geq 2^{mh(t)} - 1 \tag{4}$$
$$\forall n \in \mathbb{N}, \ \forall i \in \mathbb{N} \mid 2^i \leq n < 2^{i+1} \Rightarrow \lfloor \log_2(n) \rfloor = i \tag{5}$$

Given these properties, the proof of (2) is immediate: By (3) and (4) it follows that $2^{mh(t)} \leq nc(t) + 1 < 2^{mh(t)+1}$, and by (5) we conclude that $\lfloor \log_2(nc(t) + 1) \rfloor = mh(t)$.

Figure 1 shows the proof written in LH. It is worth noticing that, due to the complexity of the proof, it is impossible to automate it without guiding the proof through the use of proof combinators up to a point where the SMT-solver can take over and determine whether the proof is correct.

The proof of property (1) requires more effort due to the definition of `log2C`, the ceiling of the logarithm. Since `log2C` distinguishes cases based on the result of `log2F`, one needs to associate the unfolding of the function with another property in order to work with a concrete result rather than a raw application. To achieve this, we state two other properties that relate a tree's height with its number of nodes.

$$balanced(t) \wedge mh(t) = h(t) \Rightarrow 2^{\lfloor \log_2(nc(t)+1) \rfloor} = nc(t) + 1 \tag{6}$$

$$balanced(t) \wedge mh(t) + 1 = h(t) \Rightarrow 2^{\lfloor \log_2(nc(t)+1) \rfloor} < nc(t) + 1 \tag{7}$$

Using these properties, we can perform case analysis in the proof of (1) replacing the function call to `log2C` by the corresponding case. Once this replacement is performed, we are able to reach the desired result. The complete proof in LH can be found in Fig. 2.

```
{-@ prop_1 :: t : BTree a -> { log2C (nc t + 1) == h t } @-}
prop_1     = ()
prop_1 t | h t == mh t = log2C n == h t ? prop_6 t
         === log2F (nc t + 1) == h t ? prop_2 t
         === mh t == h t ***
         | h t == mh t + 1 = log2C n == h t ? prop_7 t
         === log2F (nc t + 1) + 1 == h t ? prop_2 t
         === mh t + 1 == h t ***
```

Fig. 2. Proof of property (1).

4   Braun Trees

Braun trees [2,8] are binary trees that support efficient element access by natural number index. Each node implicitly corresponds to a position determined by the path taken from the root. To access the element at position i, one considers the binary representation of i. Starting from the least significant bit, a bit value of 0 indicates that the left child should be followed, while a bit value of 1 indicates the right child. This process continues until the most significant bit is reached, at which point the desired element is found. For instance, Fig. 3 shows a Braun tree with 6 elements. We omit the node values, but we do include their indices and their binary representation.

Due to their structure, Braun trees provide an efficient representation of functional arrays, supporting logarithmic-time access and updates. Additionally,

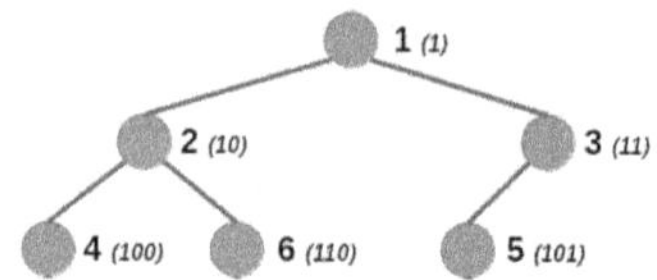

Fig. 3. Example of a Braun Tree.

their balanced nature allows them to grow or shrink with minimal cost. The key
structural invariant of Braun trees states that, at every node, the left subtree is
always either equal in size to the right subtree or larger by exactly one element.
This invariant guarantees that the tree remains balanced, maintaining a depth
of $O(\log_2 n)$.

We define Braun trees by extending the tree structure of the previous section
with the structural invariant.

```
{-@ type Braun a = { t : Tree a | braun t } @-}
type Braun a = Tree a

{-@ reflect braun @-}
{-@ braun :: Tree a -> Bool @-}
braun (Node _ l r) = (nc l == nc r || nc l == nc r + 1) &&
                     braun l && braun r
braun Nil          = True
```

Element access is based on the binary representation of the index. To access
a node whose binary index ends in a 1, the structure must already contain the
corresponding node where that bit is 0. This ensures that the path exists in the
tree. As a result, the left subtree always contains the same number of elements
as the right subtree, or at most one more.

An interesting property states that Braun trees are balanced trees.

$$braun(t) \Rightarrow balanced(t)$$

The proof is by induction on the structure of Braun trees. The `Nil` case is
immediate. For the inductive case, we establish the following auxiliary property
that relates the **balanced** predicate with the absolute value of the difference in
the number of nodes between the immediate subtrees of a non-empty tree.

$$balanced(l) \wedge balanced(r) \wedge |\, nc(l) - nc(r)\,| \leq 1 \Rightarrow balanced(Node\, x\, l\, r) \qquad (8)$$

The proof of (8) proceeds by case analysis over whether the subtree node counts
are exact powers of two, and whether the maximum and minimum heights of the
resulting tree `Node x l r` are derived from the left or right subtree. In each case,
the goal is to show that the difference between the maximum and the minimum
height of the tree is at most one. The proof uses properties (3) and (4) to convert
the structural properties of the subtrees into logarithmic expressions. The final
step in each branch applies the fact that the difference between the ceiling and

floor of a logarithm (or between two such expressions from similar-sized subtrees) is at most one.

Using (8) it becomes straightforward to relate braun trees to balanced trees. The complete proof in LH can be found in Fig. 4.

```
{-@ braun_is_balanced :: t : Braun a -> { balanced t } @-}
braun_is_balanced                       = ()
braun_is_balanced t@(    v l r) = balanced t
   === (balanced l && balanced r && h t - mh t <= 1)
       ? braun_is_balanced l
   === (balanced r &&  h t - mh t <= 1)
       ? braun_is_balanced r
   === h t - mh t <= 1 ? prop_8 v l r ***
```

Fig. 4. Proof of balance of Braun Trees.

Directly from the structural property, it is possible to prove that in a Braun tree `nc t` satisfies the following inequalities:

$$\mathrm{braun}(t) \Rightarrow 2^{h(t)-1} \le \mathrm{nc}(t) < 2^{h(t)} \tag{9}$$

A proof of this property in Why3 is presented by Filliâtre [1]. We were able to replicate it in LH by means of the following lemmas:

```
{-@ inv_size :: l : Braun a -> r : {Braun a | nc r <= nc l}
            -> {h l >= h r}

    type BraunGE a N = { t : Braun a | nc t >= N }

    inv_height1 :: t:BraunGE a 1 -> {pow2 (h t - 1) <= nc t}
    inv_height2 :: t:BraunGE a 1 -> {pow2 h t > nc t} @-}
```

Both `inv_height` lemmas establish the lower and upper bound on the `nc` function, respectively, while `inv_size` helps decide on the unfolding of the `h t` function. Compared to Why3, LH struggles more with reasoning about inequalities involving `pow2` and `nc`. We have to guide the proof manually until reaching a point where an inductive step can be applied, allowing LH to complete the verification; something that Why3 is often able to handle automatically.

4.1 Arrays

Having defined Braun trees, we now turn to using them as a foundation for implementing functional arrays. Our development on functional arrays is motivated by the one presented by Nipkow and Sewell [6].

```
{-@ type Array a = Braun a @-}
type Array a = Braun a
```

Associated with this structure, we define the following operations on arrays: `lookup`, `update`, `adds`, `len`, and `list`. As we develop these functions, it is desirable to establish their key correctness properties. LH facilitates this process by allowing us to specify and verify invariants relative to these functions.

For instance, using the refinement type `ArrayGE a n`, which represents an array with at least `n` elements, we can restrict the `lookup` function to ensure that the index we are looking for is always present in the array:

```
{-@ type ArrayGE a N = BraunGE a N @-}
{-@ lookup :: { n: Nat | n > 0 } -> ArrayGE a n -> a @-}
lookup 1 t@(Node v _ _) = v
lookup n t@(Node v l r) | even n     = lookup (div n 2) l
                        | otherwise = lookup (div n 2) r
```

However, when attempting to prove the correctness of this definition, a challenge arises: LH cannot automatically infer that if the index is not even, then `nc r >= div n 2`, even when the overall condition `nc (Node v l r)>= n` holds. This limitation stems from the definition of Braun trees, which enforces a left-heavy balance. Although this invariant guarantees that the right subtree is populated when needed, LH is not able to deduce this implicitly. To assist the SMT-solver in reasoning about parity and branching, we explicitly promote the `even` function into the refinement logic.

```
{-@ reflect even @-}
even i = i 'mod' 2 == 0
```

By combining this reflection with `PLE`, we allow LH to reason about parity, enabling it to correctly deduce the shape and size of subtrees during recursive calls. `PLE` is a key part of this proof since the solver needs the unfolding to correctly resolve the invariants.

This promotion will be the basis for all subsequent operations, as they rely on similar structural reasoning.

The `update` function either modifies an existing element or extends the array by one element, with the following refinement type:

```
{-@ type ArrayNON1 a N I
  = {arr : Array a | (I <= N => nc arr == N) &&
                     (I == N+1 => nc arr == N+1)} @-}

{-@ update :: {n:Nat | n>0} -> a -> arr:ArrayGE a {n-1}
          -> ArrayNON1 a {nc arr} {n} @-}
update :: Int -> a -> Array a -> Array a
update _ x Nil              = singleton x
update 1 x t@(Node v l r) = makeT x l r
update n x t@(Node v l r)
  | even n     = makeT v (update (div n 2) x l) r
  | otherwise = makeT v l (update (div (n-1) 2) x r)
```

Again we make sure that the element we want to update is in the structure by using `ArrayGE`. The return type `ArrayNON1` preserves the Braun invariant limiting the number of nodes to either the same number or increased by exactly one.

Functions `makeT` and `singleton` have the following annotations in the refinement logic:

```
{-@ type ArrayN a N = { arr : Array a | nc arr == N } @-}

{-@ makeT :: v : a -> l : Array a
          -> r : {Array a | nc l == nc r || nc l == nc r + 1}
          -> t : ArrayN a { 1 + nc l + nc r }    @-}

{-@ singleton :: a -> ArrayN a 1 @-}
```

The `singleton` function provides a simple way to construct a leaf node. In contrast, `makeT` is particularly useful when building more complex trees.

The `adds` operation extends an array by adding the elements of a list `xs` at the end. The size of the resulting array is then `n + length xs`.

```
{-@ reflect adds @-}
{-@ adds :: xs : [a] -> n : Nat -> ArrayN a n
         -> ArrayN a { n + length xs } @-}
adds :: [a] -> Int -> Array a -> Array a
adds []      _ t = t
adds (x:xs) n t = adds xs (n+1) (update (n+1) x t)
```

The `len` operation is straightforward, as it simply returns the node count.

```
{-@ len :: arr : Array a -> {n : Nat | nc arr == n} @-}
len arr = nc arr
```

Lastly, we would like to be able to transform arrays to lists; for this we define the function `list`. This function is governed by the following invariant:

```
{-@ list :: arr:Array a -> {xs:[a] | nc arr == length xs} @-}
list Nil         = []
list (Node x l r) =  x : splice (list l) (list r)

{-@ reflect splice @-}
{-@ splice :: xs:[a] -> ys:[a]
       -> zs : {[a] | length zs == length xs + length ys} @-}
splice :: [a] -> [a] -> [a]
```

The type `{ xs : [a] | nc arr == length xs }` states that the output list `xs` contains exactly `nc arr` elements of type `a`. In this case the splice function alternates elements of the lists so the sorting is correct.

So far it has not been necessary to rely on the theorem-proving capabilities of LH. However, here we are faced with a difficulty: while we can verify that the sizes match, the next natural question is whether the order of the elements in the list corresponds to their traversal order in the tree. To verify this, two alternatives can be considered. The first one is to enrich the refinement type of the function by extending the invariant with an explicit notion of element order, allowing LH to check the alignment between the tree and list positions. The second alternative is to shift the problem towards the theorem-proving capabilities, where we can encode and prove a separate property that establishes the alignment. The first alternative corresponds to a correct-by-construction approach, whereas the second one a more traditional verification approach.

We finally chose the second alternative. We had previously explored the first one for other functions, but found that it significantly increased both complexity and verbosity of the code. In particular, maintaining the necessary invariants required adding new components to our structure, as well as implementing auxiliary types and helper functions to carry additional information throughout recursive transformations. While this was sometimes partially successful, it made the codebase more difficult to manage and less modular.

4.2 Functional Correctness of Array Operations

In this section, we validate the invariants proposed in [6] for the array operations introduced in the previous subsection. The following properties are automatically valid, essentially because they are encoded as part of the refinement types of the respective functions:

$(IA1)$ $length(list(t)) = nc(t)$

$(IA2)$ $braun(t) \wedge n \in [1, nc(t)] \Rightarrow nc(update(n, x, t)) = nc(t)$

$(IA3)$ $braun(t) \wedge n \in [1, nc(t)] \Rightarrow braun(update(n, x, t))$

$(IA4)$ $braun(t) \Rightarrow nc(update(nc(t) + 1, x, t)) = nc(t) + 1$

$(IA5)$ $braun(t) \Rightarrow braun(update(nc(t) + 1, x, t))$

$(IA6)$ $braun(t)$
$$\Rightarrow nc(adds(xs, nc(t), t)) = nc(t) + length(xs) \wedge braun(adds(xs, nc(t), t))$$

Invariant (IA1) is encoded in the refinement type of `list`. Invariants (IA2) through (IA5) are proved in the implementation of `update`, and (IA6) is checked by `adds`.

On the other hand, several other invariants require additional guidance for the SMT-solver to be proved. These are verified using equational reasoning with proof combinators:

$(IA7)$ $braun(t) \wedge i < nc(t) \Rightarrow list(t) \ !! \ i = lookup(i + 1\,t)$

$(IA8)$ $braun(t) \Rightarrow list(update(nc(t) + 1, x, t)) = list(t) +\!+ [x]$

$(IA9)$ $braun(t) \Rightarrow list(adds(xs, nc(t), t)) = list(t) +\!+ xs$

$(IA10)$ $braun(t) \wedge n \in [1, nc(t)] \Rightarrow list(update(n, x, t)) = list(t)[n - 1 := x]$

An expression `xs !! i` denotes list indexing, while `xs[i := x]` denotes the list `xs` with the i-th element replaced by `x` (positions in a list start from zero).

We start with (IA7), which states the alignment that exists between the tree positions and those at the list that is obtained with the `list` function.

```
{-@ ia7 :: arr: Array a -> n: { Nat | n < nc arr }
        -> {(list arr) !! n == lookup (n+1) arr} @-}
ia7 :: Eq a => Array a -> Int -> Proof
```

The idea of the proof is inspired by the one presented by Nipkow and Sewell [6]. To establish that the list and the tree share the same element order, we require a way to proceed recursively through the tree while traversing the list in parallel. Given that the result of the `list` function is constructed by concatenating the root element to the result of the `splice` operation applied to the recursive calls of `list` on the subtrees, we can associate the choice of a branch in the tree with a corresponding segment of the list based on the parity of the index `n`. In this way, the recursive descent into the tree is naturally aligned with the decomposition of the list.

We then establish the following property; assume $length(xs) > 0$.

$$n < length(xs) + length(ys) \wedge \mid length(xs) - length(ys) \mid \leq 1$$
$$\Rightarrow splice(xs, ys) \mathbin{!!} n = (\text{if } even(n) \text{ then } xs \text{ else } ys) \mathbin{!!} (div\, n\, 2)$$

Now we are able to rely on **PLE** to handle most of the proof. Once we structure the recursion properly and reach the inductive step, the SMT-solver is able to finish the proof without any assistance. With this result, we are able to successfully synchronize the recursive progress on both the list and tree, enabling LH to complete the proof inductively.

We now turn to the proof of Invariant (IA8):

```
{-@ ia8 :: arr:Array a -> x:a
        -> {list (update (nc arr + 1) x arr)==list arr++[x]} @-}
ia8 :: Eq a => Array a -> Int -> Proof
```

To prove this property, we must perform a case analysis based on the parity of `nc arr + 1`, as this determines the path taken by the `update` function. In case `nc arr + 1` is even, we can immediately apply the inductive hypothesis, reducing the recursive call to a list. This leads us to the following intermediate equality:

$$splice(list(l) + \!\!+ [x], list(r)) = splice(list(l), list(r)) + \!\!+ [x]$$

Similarly, in case `nc t + 1` is odd, we must prove the following:

$$splice(list(l), list(r) + \!\!+ [x]) = splice(list(l), list(r)) + \!\!+ [x]$$

In both cases, we establish the result by proving the respective equalities as separate lemmas. Each lemma calls the other after one step of unfolding, thereby completing the proof by mutual induction. Once these lemmas are verified, the overall property is established.

Invariant (IA9) ensures that `adds` behaves like standard list append:

```
{-@ ia9 :: arr:Array a -> xs:[a]
        -> {list (adds xs (nc arr) arr)==list arr ++ xs} @-}
ia9 :: Eq a => Array a -> Int -> Proof
```

The main challenge is the recursive nature of `adds`, which iterates over the input list until reaching the empty list. To proceed, we invoke the inductive hypothesis to replace each recursive call to `adds` with a call to `update`. We then can leverage the property previously proven for `update`, thereby eliminating it in favor of list operations. At that point, the goal reduces to proving the following standard properties of list concatenation: $xs ++ [] = xs$ which is trivial and $list(t) ++ [x] ++ xs = list(t) ++ (x : xs)$. Once these auxiliary lemmas are established, LH is able to complete the proof automatically.

The last property we verify is (IA10), which reduces to proving the following:

```
{-@ ia10 :: v:a -> n:{Nat | n >= 1} -> arr:ArrayGE a n
      -> {list (update n v arr)==change (n-1) v (list arr)} @-}
ia10 :: Eq a => a -> Int -> Array a -> Proof
```

In the proof of this property, it is possible to quickly apply the inductive step and eliminate the `update` operation from the reasoning. The main difficulty stems from the fact that, regardless of the parity of the updated index, the recursive descent in the tree always yields an even index until the base case is reached at 1 or 2. To effectively complete the proof, one needs to establish additional properties about list updates, particularly how updates propagate through the `splice` operation.

$$n \geq 2 \wedge n \leq len(xs) + len(ys) + 1 \wedge even(n)$$
$$\Rightarrow \; splice(xs[div\, n\, 2 - 1 := v], ys) = splice(xs, ys)[n - 2 := v]$$
$$n \geq 2 \wedge n \leq len(xs) + len(ys) \wedge even(n)$$
$$\Rightarrow \; splice(xs, ys[div\, n\, 2 - 1 := v]) = splice(xs, ys)[n - 1 := v]$$
$$n \geq 2 \wedge n \leq len(xs) + len(ys) \wedge \neg even(n)$$
$$\Rightarrow \; splice(xs, ys[div\, n\, 2 - 1 := v]) = splice(xs, ys)[n - 1 := v]$$

Each of these properties use the other to prove that the induction is done correctly. With these auxiliary properties we are able to reason about the list structure sufficiently for the SMT-solver to verify the desired property.

4.3   Flexible Arrays

Flexible arrays are data structures that support dynamic growth and shrinkage at both ends, allowing elements to be efficiently added or removed from either the front or the back. We extend our array structure with four operations: `add_lo`,

`add_hi`, `del_lo`, and `del_hi`. These functions provide the necessary functionality
to manipulate the array from both ends while preserving its structural invariants.

Appending an element to the end of the array is already supported by `update`.
Thus, implementing `add_hi` amounts to calling `update` with the current size of
the array to append the new element.

The `add_lo` function, which inserts an element at the beginning, requires
rebalancing the tree to preserve the Braun invariant. This is done by recursively
inserting the existing root into the right subtree and swapping the branches:

```
{-@ add_lo :: x:a -> arr:Array a -> ArrayN a {nc arr + 1} @-}
add_lo x Nil           = singleton x
add_lo x (Node v l r) = makeT x (add_lo v r) l
```

Since the `Array` type guarantees the Braun property, the required invariants
are enforced by construction.

To implement `del_lo`, which removes the first element (i.e., the root), we
merge the left and right subtrees. The `merge` function must reverse the effect of
`add_lo` to maintain structural integrity:

```
{-@ del_lo :: arr : Array a
     -> {res:Array a | nc arr > 0 => nc res == nc arr -1} @-}
del_lo Nil           = Nil
del_lo (Node _ l r) = merge l r

{-@ reflect merge @-}
{-@ merge :: arr1 : Array a
          -> { arr2 : Array a | nc arr2 == nc arr1 ||
                                nc arr1 == nc arr2 + 1 }
          -> ArrayN a { nc arr1 + nc arr2 } @-}
merge :: Array a -> Array a -> Array a
```

Finally, the `del_hi` operation removes the last element by navigating to it
and replacing it with `Nil`. The type signature ensures that the resulting tree has
exactly one fewer node than the input:

```
{-@ del_hi :: n : Nat -> ArrayN a n
           -> { a : Array a | n > 0 => nc a == n-1 } @-}
del_hi _ Nil       = Nil
del_hi n (Node v l r)
          | n == 1         = Nil
          | not (even n) = makeT v l (del_hi (div n 2) r)
          | otherwise    = makeT v (del_hi (div n 2) l) r
```

4.4   Functional Correctness of Flexible Array Operations

Following [6], we validate the following invariants for flexible arrays.

(IF1) $nc(add\_lo(x,t)) = nc(t) + 1$ (IF5) $braun(Node\ x\ l\ r) \Rightarrow braun(merge(l,\ r))$

(IF2) $nc(t) > 0$ (IF6) $braun(t) \Rightarrow braun(del\_hi(nc(t),\ t))$

$\quad \Rightarrow nc(del\_lo(t)) = nc(t) - 1$

(IF3) $nc(t) > 0$ (IF7) $braun(t) \Rightarrow braun(add\_lo(x,\ t))$

$\quad \Rightarrow nc(del\_hi(nc(t), t)) = nc(t) - 1$

(IF4) $nc(add\_hi(x,t)) = nc(t) + 1$ (IF8) $braun(t) \Rightarrow braun(del\_lo(t))$

Invariants (IF1) through (IF3) are encoded in the output types of the functions. Similarly, invariants (IF5) through (IF8) are verified by setting the result type to `Array`, ensuring that the output satisfies, by construction, the structural requirements of a Braun tree. Invariant (IF4) is established by using the `ArrayNON1` type in the output of the `update` function.

Even though some properties could be directly verified through function definitions and refinement types, other invariants require more powerful reasoning. This is the case of the following invariants, which require the application of theorem-proving features:

$$(IF9)\ braun(t) \Rightarrow list(add\_lo(a,\ t)) = a : list(t)$$

$$(IF10)\ braun(Node\ x\ l\ r) \Rightarrow list(merge(l,\ r)) = splice(list(l),\ list(r))$$

$$(IF11)\ braun(t) \wedge nc(t) > 0 \Rightarrow list(del\_lo(t)) = tail(list(t))$$

$$(IF12)\ braun(t) \wedge nc(t) > 0 \Rightarrow list(del\_hi(nc(t),\ t)) = init(list(t))$$

where `tail` and `init` are the Haskell functions that return all the elements of a non-empty list except for the first one and last one, respectively.

For (IF9), we prove that inserting an element at the beginning of an array corresponds to prepending that element to the list representation.

```
{-@ if9 :: x: a -> arr: Array a
       -> {  x : list (add_lo x arr) == list arr } @-}
if9 :: Eq a => a -> Array a -> Proof
```

In this case, unfolding `add_lo` and reaching its inductive step is sufficient for LH to automatically complete the proof without additional guidance.

Property (IF10) associates the merging of trees with the `splice` operation:

```
{-@ if10 :: arr1 : Array a
        -> arr2:{Array a | nc arr2 == nc arr1 ||
                           nc arr1 == nc arr2 + 1 }
        -> { splice (list arr1)(list arr2)
                 == list (merge arr1 arr2) } @-}
if10 :: Eq a => Array a -> Array a -> Proof
```

In this case, LH is able to solve the proof automatically.

Property (IF11) states that converting the result of `del_lo` to a list yields the same result as taking the tail of the list obtained from the original array:

```
{-@ if11 :: arr : Array a
         -> {tail (list arr) == list (del_lo arr)} @-}
if11 :: Eq a => Array a -> Proof
```

Here we encounter a challenge: on one side we are doing recursion on a list, and on the other side, on a tree that is being merged. The proof relies on (IF10).

Finally, (IF12) states that removing the last element from a Braun tree corresponds to dropping the last element from its list representation.

```
{-@ if12 :: arr:  { Array a | nc arr > 0 }
        -> {init (list arr) == list (del_hi (nc arr) arr)} @-}
if12 :: Eq a => Array a -> Proof
```

The proof again relies on reasoning about the `splice` operation. In the inductive step, after unfolding `del_hi`, the proof splits into two cases based on the parity of the node count of the tree. Although we can successfully reduce the operation, this is not enough for LH to complete the proof. It is necessary to establish the following two properties, which, based on the parity of the sum of the list lengths, state that the application of `init` to a `splice` can be reduced to its application to one of its argument lists:

$$even(len(xs) + len(ys)) \Rightarrow init(splice(xs, ys)) = splice(xs, init(ys))$$
$$\neg\, even(len(xs) + len(ys)) \Rightarrow init(splice(xs, ys)) = splice(init(xs), ys)$$

5   Related Work

Previous work has explored the formal verification of Braun trees and other balanced data structures in various proof assistants. However, to our knowledge, this is the first formal verification of Braun trees using LH. Nipkow and Sewell [6] provide a comprehensive Isabelle/HOL development, including correctness and complexity proofs for Braun tree operations. Their work inspired our LH formalization, although we restrict our focus to the structural invariants and functional correctness of the array operations, excluding most of their linear-time optimizations. From an implementation point of view, the main difference with the development in Isabelle is LH's ability to embed proofs directly within function definitions, rather than requiring all properties to be proved separately as theorems. In fact, a relevant feature of LH is the possibility to write proofs in the same language as the final programs. This provides a significant safety benefit: any modification to the code can be rechecked automatically, without needing to first prove the logic in a separate proof language. Furthermore, this integration ensures that all proof-related information remains within the same codebase and incorporated it to the development process.

Filliâtre [1] implemented a variant of Braun trees to model heaps in Why3, proving their correctness with respect to a priority queue specification. Although

Why3 and LH differ in underlying logic and methodology, both aim to express structural invariants through annotations. Compared to Filliâtre's implementation, the `inv_height` property required only 14 lines of Why3 code and almost no proof guidance. In contrast, our LH proof of the same property spanned 34 lines, most of which were dedicated to guiding the system towards the correct reasoning. On the other hand, cases like `fast_size`, an operation introduced by Okasaki [7] and formally verified by Filliâtre (not included in this paper due to lack of space), required us only the introduction of a simple invariant at the logic level (which is automatically verified by LH). This allowed us to obtain results very similar to those of Why3, with minimal additional effort.

Unlike other approaches that only check properties externally, our implementation encodes many function invariants, and the pre- and post-conditions that preserve them, directly at the refinement type level. As a result, functions like `lookup` and `update` cannot be called with an invalid index, nor can any operation be applied to a tree that does not satisfy the Braun tree invariant.

Okasaki [7] and Nipkow and Sewell [6] have also explored alternative definitions of some of the array operations in order to improve their performance. Our formalization includes the implementation of these efficient operations, but we do not include them here due to lack of space. They can be found in our online repository (https://gitlab.fing.edu.uy/felipe.de.leon/brauntrees).

In the LH ecosystem, Vazou et al. [13] demonstrated the use of LH to verify properties of red-black trees. Their work validates that refinement types can express and enforce non-trivial invariants such as balancedness. Although they demonstrate such properties, the version of LH they used lacked both the `reflect` directive and the proof combinators that our solution takes advantage of to a large extent.

Other efforts have been made to formalize related data structures in LH. Rondo [9], for example, presented an implementation of AVL trees purely using `measures`. We experimented with this approach during our development, and while it yielded good results in some cases, it often required substantial auxiliary code and structures. In comparison, a hybrid approach, leveraging both measures and reflected functions, has provided significantly better results by combining the strengths of both techniques.

Finally, while most work involving LH focuses on theoretical developments or isolated examples, our contribution takes a more practical approach by using the tool to replicate and validate existing proofs in a use case that is simple enough to be accessible, yet rich enough to be non-trivial.

6   Conclusions and Future Work

During the course of this work, we experimented in a non-trivial use case with the different capabilities offered by LH to formalize and verify program invariants. LH directives proved to be particularly useful for automatically verifying structural properties, such as those related to balanced trees and the Braun condition. In some cases, the proofs were remarkably straightforward, with the solver handling constraint enforcement automatically. A striking case is, for example, the one where the simply promotion of a single function like `even` enabled the solver to reason effectively about parity.

However, in other cases, particularly those involving non-trivial mathematical properties such as logarithmic bounds, considerable development effort was required to assist the solver in reasoning through the proof. This also marks a significant shift in the programming paradigm, as developers must adopt the mindset of a theorem prover, along with the associated learning curve that comes with understanding and effectively using these formal verification tools.

With respect to LH's reasoning capabilities, we initially aimed to heavily rely on its PLE feature to automate much of the verification effort. While this was effective for simple local properties, we found it insufficient for more complex proofs that lacked straightforward recursion patterns suitable for unfolding. Nonetheless, PLE remained a valuable tool, even if its applicability was more limited than we had originally expected.

In summary, LH proved to be a flexible and powerful tool for formal program verification. While it is less expressive than full proof assistants, its seamless integration with Haskell enables verification to become a natural part of the development workflow.

We envision two main directions for future work. The first involves to further continue with the formalization of operations on Braun trees. In particular, we have already begun the formalization of some of the efficient operations on Braun trees presented by Okasaki [7]. Another interesting structure to analyze is the Braun-tree-based implementation of priority queues, following the works of Nipkow and Sewell [6] and Filliâtre [1].

The second direction focuses on reworking the definition of functions and proofs using an intrinsically-typed definition of Braun trees, where the structural invariant is encoded as part of the data type definition (and not as an external predicate). We have already experimented with this technique in our LH implementation of AVL trees [4,5].

References

1. Filliâtre, J.C.: Purely applicative heaps implemented with Braun trees. https:// toccata.gitlabpages.inria.fr/toccata/gallery/braun_trees.en.html (2015). formal proof development in Why3
2. Hoogerwoord, R.R.: A logarithmic implementation of flexible arrays. In: Bird, R.S., Morgan, C., Woodcock, J. (eds.) Mathematics of Program Construction, Second International Conference, Oxford, U.K., June 29 - July 3, 1992, Proceedings. Lecture Notes in Computer Science, vol. 669, pp. 191–207. Springer (1992)
3. Jhala, R.: Writing Specifications liquidhaskell docs. https://ucsd-progsys.github.io/liquidhaskell/specifications/ (2020). Accessed 15 May 2024
4. de León Arias, F.: Estudio del lenguaje LiquidHaskell. Final degree project, Facultad de Ingeniería, Universidad de la República (Uruguay) (2024). https://www.colibri.udelar.edu.uy/jspui/handle/20.500.12008/47485
5. de León Arias, F.: Implementation of AVL Trees in LiquidHaskell (2024). https://gitlab.fing.edu.uy/felipe.de.leon/liquid-structures/-/blob/main/src/AVLTrees.hs

6. Nipkow, T., Sewell, T.: Proof pearl: Braun trees. In: Proceedings of the 9th ACM SIGPLAN International Conference on Certified Programs and Proofs, pp. 18–31. CPP 2020, Association for Computing Machinery, New York, NY, USA (2020). https://doi.org/10.1145/3372885.3373834
7. Okasaki, C.: Three algorithms on Braun trees. J. Funct. Program. **7**(6), 661–666 (1997). https://doi.org/10.1017/S0956796897002876
8. Paulson, L.C.: ML for the Working Programmer, 2nd edn. Cambridge University Press, Cambridge (1996)
9. Rondon, P., Vazou, N.: Programming with refinement types: Liquidhaskell tutorial. https://ucsd-progsys.github.io/liquidhaskell-tutorial/book.pdf. Accessed 24 May 2025
10. Vazou, N., Breitner, J., Kunkel, R., Van Horn, D., Hutton, G.: Theorem proving for all: equational reasoning in liquid Haskell (functional pearl). In: Proceedings of the 11th ACM SIGPLAN International Symposium on Haskell, pp. 132–144. Haskell 2018, Association for Computing Machinery, New York, NY, USA (2018). https://doi.org/10.1145/3242744.3242756
11. Vazou, N., Breitner, J., Kunkel, W., Horn, D.V., Hutton, G.: Reasoning about programs. https://goto.ucsd.edu/~nvazou/theorem-proving-for-all/02-Reasoning-About-Programs.html (2013). Accessed 15 May 2024
12. Vazou, N., Rondon, P.M., Jhala, R.: Abstract refinement types. In: Felleisen, M., Gardner, P. (eds.) Programming Languages and Systems, pp. 209–228. Springer, Berlin Heidelberg, Berlin, Heidelberg (2013)
13. Vazou, N., Seidel, E., Jhala, R.: LiquidHaskell: experience with refinement types in the real world. In: Proceedings of the 2014 ACM SIGPLAN Symposium on Haskell, pp. 39–51. Haskell '14, Association for Computing Machinery, New York, NY, USA (2014). https://doi.org/10.1145/2633357.2633366

HOL4P4.EXE: A Formally Verified P4 Software Switch

Didrik Lundberg[1,2]($\boxtimes$) and Roberto Guanciale[1,3]

[1] KTH Royal Institute of Technology, Lindstedtsvägen 5, 100 44 Stockholm, Sweden
{didrikl,robertog}@kth.se
[2] Saab AB, Nettovägen 6, 175 41 Järfälla, Sweden
[3] Digital Futures, Osquars Backe 5, 100 44 Stockholm, Sweden

Abstract. The emergence of programmable network elements and their usage in critical infrastructure is increasing the demand for formal guarantees of their correctness. This paper presents the first P4 software switch connected by proof to a formal semantics. This is accomplished by adjusting and optimizing the HOL4P4 semantics to create an efficient interpreter that can be compiled using the verified CakeML compiler. We demonstrate practical performance in a set of experiments, achieving several orders of magnitude improvement in throughput over existing semantics-based interpreters, with only small performance penalties compared to the BMv2 reference switch written in C++.

Keywords: P4 · Theorem Proving · Formal Verification

1 Introduction

Software-defined networking gives hardware owners the power to fine-tune the data plane processing in a protocol-independent manner. The typical use case for leveraging this flexibility is to gain a rapid development cycle (as opposed to that of non-programmable hardware) and to support specialized infrastructure with custom performance and security solutions. The P4 language is the de facto standard for programmable network elements, and P4 compilers target a variety of platforms from terabit-bandwidth switches [8] to network interface controller (NIC) cards. In addition, P4 programs can run on commodity CPUs by various means [21].

When executing a high-level language like P4, the compilers, interpreters, and runtimes involved may deviate from the language's intended semantics or introduce bugs, especially if they are complex, written in an unsafe language, and heavily performance-optimized. The goal of this work is to address these problems by developing a formally verified P4 software switch, hereafter referred to as HOL4P4.EXE[1]. A *verified software switch* is a provably correct implementation of P4 programs and architecture models according to a high-level formal semantics.

---

[1] The source code is available in the HOL4P4 Github repository https://github.com/kth-step/HOL4P4 at the tag **VSTTE2025**.

C. Pit-Claudel and K. Kosaian (Eds.): VSTTE 2025, LNCS 16499, pp. 71–82, 2026.
https://doi.org/10.1007/978-3-032-27340-6_5

Our main strategy is to compile the HOL4P4 semantics, a formal semantics of the P4 language developed in the HOL4 interactive theorem prover, into an executable interpreter using the CakeML verified compiler. This enables us to bridge the gap between formal verification and practical deployment of P4 software switches. This paper makes four key contributions:

First, we modify the original HOL4P4 semantics to be compatible with CakeML extraction and update the symbolic executor to enable end-to-end proofs of program behavior at the machine code level.

Second, we profile the resulting interpreter and identify several performance bottlenecks in the CakeML-generated code. Guided by these insights, we develop an optimized version that significantly reduces extraction time and yields a more efficient binary. This offers practical guidance on building performant interpreters via executable semantics.

Third, we extend the verified interpreter with a raw-socket FFI, resulting in a usable software switch. We further integrate it with Mininet [10], demonstrating that HOL4P4.EXE can operate within realistic testing environments.

Finally, We evaluate HOL4P4.EXE side-by-side with existing solutions, showing that it outperforms current semantics-based implementations and scales well with increasing packet sizes.

HOL4P4.EXE is the first P4 software switch with formal verification guarantees. Our results demonstrate that verified systems can achieve practical performance, advancing the goal of high-assurance networking.

2   Related Work

We use HOL4P4 [1] as formal semantics of P4. HOL4P4 is a heapless semantics written in the interactive theorem prover (ITP) HOL4 and has an executable formulation, that is, a version that can be evaluated in the ITP, computing the result of running a P4 program. To facilitate verification of P4 programs, HOL4P4 has been extended with a symbolic executor [14]. In this work we also use CakeML [9], a verified compiler implemented in HOL4 which compiles the CakeML language, a dialect of Standard ML. CakeML is also capable of verified extraction of CakeML code from HOL4 definitions.

There are a number of software switches that enable running a P4 program on a regular CPU. BMv2 [18] is a "reference P4 software switch implementation". However, unlike HOL4P4.EXE, BMv2 is not based on a formal semantics. Petr4 [4] is a P4 semantics and formalization in OCaml. There exists a version of petr4 which can also be compiled and used as a software switch, e.g. with Mininet [6], making it directly comparable to HOL4P4.EXE. The petr4 semantics has also been ported to the Coq ITP [4,19,26], however there is no formal connection between the petr4 software switch and the ITP semantics.

The Coq ecosystem also includes the verified compiler CompCert [10], and a fully verified C code extraction mechanism from Coq, which does not currently exist, would offer a similar pathway to a verified switch as the one presented in this paper.

PfComp [3] is another work that applies both theorem-proving and verified compilation to networking. It uses Coq to construct a verified compiler from firewall policies to Clight, which can in turn be compiled using CompCert. In contrast to the P4 programs used to program HOL4P4.EXE, the policy language of PfComp does not include packet parsing, modification and deparsing, nor outcomes beyond acceptance or rejection.

In addition to the ITP-based verification tools [5,14,19,26,27], multiple non-proof-producing tools have been made to verify P4 programs [11,17,23]. Verification tools are complementary to a verified switch implementation, whose main purpose is to transfer verified properties from source code to machine code.

3   System Description

The core of HOL4P4.EXE is a verified P4 interpreter, obtained by adapting the existing HOL4P4 semantics and architectural models (V1Model and eBPF), and then compiling the semantics function via the verified CakeML compiler. The main challenge lies in refining the semantics to support CakeML extraction while preserving the soundness of the verification tools, in identifying bottlenecks and optimizations that can guide the development of efficient executable semantics, and integrating the interpreter in a way that minimizes the trusted computing base (TCB). The version of the semantics with the optimizations described in Sect. 3.1 is called the *optimized semantics* in the rest of the paper. We have also implemented in HOL4 a translator from the abstract syntax tree (AST) of standard HOL4P4 programs and initial states to those of the optimized semantics.

Several aspects of the HOL4P4 semantics make it a good candidate as basis for our executable interpreter. In particular, the semantics models the specific P4 calling convention, which forbids cross-function variable references, via a heapless design: as opposed to allocating local variables in a global heap, HOL4P4 keeps them in function frames that are disposed of upon function return.

Figure 1 shows an overview of HOL4P4.EXE. The verified interpreter is used together with a wrapper program in CakeML and a foreign function interface (FFI) library to communicate over Linux raw sockets to obtain a usable software switch. This paper's code contributions are shown in green: the architecture models and semantics are adapted from prior work. The parts below the dashed line exist inside the theorem prover HOL4, while the parts above it are outside.

Note that the P4 program and the table configurations are statically embedded in the final HOL4P4.EXE executable. This is achieved by extracting the HOL4 term representing the AST of the program to CakeML, which is then compiled into machine code that reconstructs the same AST at start time. As a result, the interpreter begins execution with the target P4 program already parsed and ready for packet processing.

From a usability perspective, standard P4 programs can be translated into HOL4P4 programs by using the .p4 parser functionality of petr4 [4] and feeding the JSON result to the HOL4P4 import tool. Also, while this paper only describes compilation to x86, the HOL4P4.EXE toolchain supports compilation to the RISC-V and ARMv8 ISAs.

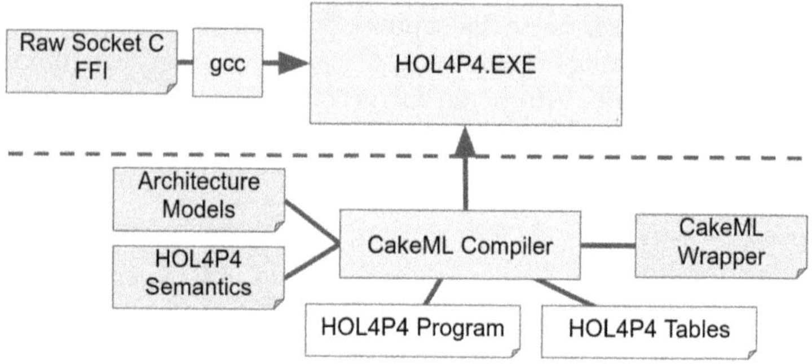

Fig. 1. HOL4P4.EXE system overview.

3.1   Refining the Semantics for CakeML

In order to make extraction to CakeML from HOL4 possible, all instances of Hilbert choice were removed from the semantics. The Hilbert choice was initially used for indefinite values of uninitialised variables. The resulting semantics zeroes all new variables, which is sound with respect to the P4 specification and indeed guaranteed by some P4 platforms. This stricter initialisation scheme preserves security properties proved by the symbolic executor, but when used as a simulator, the software switch may have more restricted behaviour than generally allowed. Moreover, the partial function definitions allowed by HOL4 were replaced by option-type functions or guarded behind checks. Partial functions may also be extractable by CakeML, but require manual proofs showing that they always yield results where they are used. A quirk of P4 is the heavy usage of bitstrings of non-standard widths (e.g., 3 or 11) and operations on these. To be able to extract the semantics for arithmetic, this was rewritten to using just bitstrings and numbers instead of fixed-width word types. The rarity of numerical computations in P4 programs means that trading off performance for generality here is not significant for overall performance in practice.

Optimized Semantics. For increasing performance, all string identifiers in the semantics and architecture models (variable names, function names, field names, parser state names, table names and string constants) were replaced by native-size words, depending on compilation target: typically 64 bits, with 32 and 16 also supported. The complete evaluation is in Sect. 4, note that the comparisons here use the same test setup.

This led to around 60% increased throughput and 30% lowered latency, fairly consistent over different programs. Most extraction times stayed constant, with only a small 20% decrease in extraction time for the AST of the largest program. In our experiments, the compilation step of HOL4P4.EXE always stayed under 20 s for all tested programs except for the string version of the largest program in Sect. 4, which took 5 m. The heapless design of the HOL4P4 semantics means that many small variable maps are used instead of one large one. Here, the asymptotic benefits of efficient implementations like red-black maps become less important compared to the association lists used by HOL4P4. However, the relative speedup gained by switching identifiers from strings to native-length words is greater when using association lists, since they require more identifier comparisons per lookup.

Another important optimization was the on-demand conversion of byte arrays to the bit representation used by HOL4P4. Since the raw socket FFI yields incoming packets as byte lists, and since only the headers (and not the data payload) is supposed to affect the program, it is more efficient and scalable to only convert the necessary bytes to bits when extracting headers and vice versa when emitting. This led to 4x the throughput of the unoptimized version for 1518-byte packets, with almost indistinguishable throughput for 64-byte packets.

The most performance-critical operation in P4 programs is table matching, where, e.g., IP addresses are matched against table entries, which may include ranges and bit masks. The HOL4P4 semantics performs these operations using the same bitstring-based definitions written for the arithmetic semantics: writing a separate implementation using 64-bit word comparisons reduced performance by half when matching against tables with 1000 range-type entries. This suggests that at least on x86-64, the HOL4P4-style bitstring comparisons are more efficient than comparisons from HOL4's theory of machine words when compiled by CakeML.

3.2   Formal Guarantees

The guarantees of CakeML apply to two stages: CakeML code extraction from HOL4 definitions and binary compilation from CakeML code.

The HOL4 definitions extracted to CakeML consist of the entire semantics, the architecture models as well as the AST of the P4 program to run: in the wrapper program, only the top-level semantics function `cake_exec` is used (on the extracted *prog* and *state*, with incoming packets added). Theorem 1 states the correctness of the extraction relative to a correspondence between CakeML and HOL4 values [15]. This step is shown with red arrows in Fig. 2.

Theorem 1. *When given an application of the CakeML HOL4P4 semantics to arguments corresponding to HOL4 terms, the CakeML operational semantics will terminate with a value that corresponds to the application of the HOL4 HOL4P4 semantics to those terms.*

The compilation guarantees also preserve the semantics of the CakeML wrapper code, as stated in Theorem 2 [9,24], a simplified and specialised version of the top-level correctness theorem of CakeML. This property relies on a few assumptions: notably, that any FFI functions written externally obey CakeML's requirements, specifically that they only write to their proper memory regions when running the binary. Regarding memory, note that CakeML includes garbage collection that is formally verified to uphold the compiler correctness theorem.

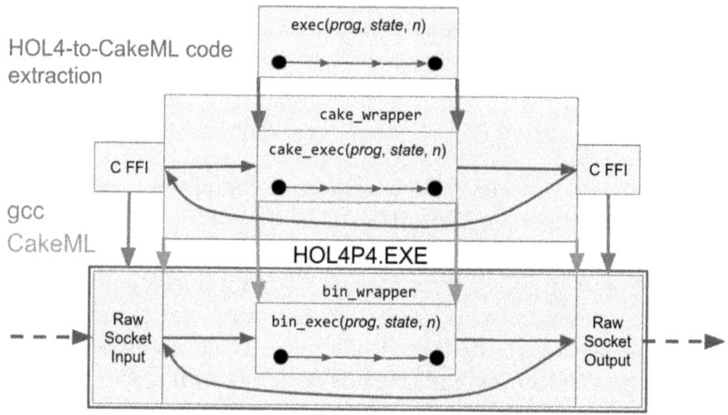

Fig. 2. Compilation overview.

Theorem 2 (Top-level compiler correctness). *The HOL4P4.EXE binary produced by a successful evaluation of the CakeML compiler function will either*

- *behave exactly according to the observable behaviour of the CakeML source code according to its semantics, or*
- *behave the same as the CakeML source code up to some point at which it terminates with an out-of-memory error.*

Table 1. Sizes of HOL4P4.EXE components

Component	Written in	Size (LoC)
FFI	C	551
Wrapper	CakeML	521
HOL4P4 executable semantics	HOL4	1650
Architecture models	HOL4	1331
Auxiliary definitions	HOL4	808
		4861

The fact that we not only enabled CakeML extraction of the executable semantics but also updated the metatheory and symbolic executor of Lundberg et al. [14] to accommodate these changes, means we can use the symbolic executor on the exact same semantics and programs that then are deployed in the verified P4 software switch. Since the verified compiler preserves functional properties, this specifically means that it preserves properties proved using the symbolic executor. Accordingly, an *end-to-end proof* is obtained in the sense that the binary fragment running the P4 program also obeys the high-level properties you have proved using the symbolic executor.

3.3   Implementation and TCB

Information about the various components is shown in Table 1. Code sizes are calculated using `cloc` and provide an indication of the size of the TCB. Components in the TCB require different degrees of trust; the FFI and the system calls have to be wholly trusted, whereas the CakeML compiler ensures the wrapper behaves according to the CakeML semantics, assuming the FFI is well-behaved. The correspondence in Theorem 1 could also be considered part of the TCB.

In theory, the FFI could get stuck in an infinite loop, or completely upend the other guarantees by writing to arbitrary memory locations. However, the raw socket FFI code size is very small, and the dependencies consist of compile-time constants and structure definitions in addition to system calls, contributing almost no additional executable code in the final binary. In addition to the listed components, standard library functions of the respective languages that are used, Linux, and its device drivers should also be considered part of the TCB.

Notably, if a P4 program is proven to satisfy a property with respect to the HOL4P4 semantics, verified compilation ensures that this property is preserved in the final binary. From the perspective of this property, the semantics and architecture model are no longer part of the TCB, as the compilation correctness theorem guarantees that the binary faithfully implements the semantics, which has been proved to guarantee the property.

The contributions in this paper also consist of changes to the existing HOL4P4 theories and tools: approximately 20000 lines of code (LoC) were added in total, according to a Git diff analysis. Around 25% of these are changes to existing theories and libraries.

For comparison, the petr4 OCaml model can be estimated to be about 12000 LoC[2] and the BMv2 model about 16500 LoC[3]. Note that these rely on the OCaml and C++ compilers, respectively, as well as any external libraries used.

4   Performance Comparisons

The main goal of this section is to isolate aspects of operation in order to obtain performance bounds and identify or rule out potential bottlenecks. Unless noted otherwise, all HOL4P4.EXE results refer to the version using the optimized semantics.

To evaluate our system experimentally, we have selected the following P4 programs, all using the V1Model architecture:

1. `port_swap.p4`: This small program extracts and emits Ethernet and IPv4 headers unchanged, and looks at the ingress port: if it is 1, the egress port is set to 2, otherwise to 1. This is meant to illustrate the baseline cost of P4 interpretation and the overhead of the basic V1Model pipeline implementation.

---

[2] Estimated using `cloc *.ml` on the `lib` directory of the latest release (0.1.3).

[3] Estimated using `cloc *.c *.cpp *.h` on the `src/bm_sim` directory of the latest release (0.15.0).

2. `vss-example.p4`: A medium-sized P4 program from the "Very Simple Switch" (VSS) example of the P4 Specification [25] which performs basic switch functionality. For these tests, it has been adapted to the V1Model architecture.
3. `fabric_border_router.p4`: A larger (2816 LoC) real-world industry program used at Google [22]. Note that HOL4P4.EXE only has placeholder models for timing-dependent externs such as meters whose real-world implementations rely on system clocks.

The sizes of the programs cover a range of P4 program sizes from minimal to real-world industry applications, and so are suitable to determine scalability. To provide context for these measurements, the minimum bandwidth listed under Zoom system requirements for a 720p HD video call is 1.2Mbps, while the minimum for a voice call is 80kbps [29]. Netflix recommends 5Mbps or higher for 1080p video streaming [16].

All measurements were performed on a laptop with an Intel® i7-8550U CPU. This involved first setting up small virtual networks in a Mininet-like fashion and configuring the environment to maximize the accuracy of the measurements, after which Pktgen-DPDK [28] was used to run test suites scripted in Lua.[4]

The closest comparable (but unverified) tool to HOL4P4.EXE is petr4[5], the only other software switch based on a formal semantics known to the authors, written in OCaml. HOL4P4.EXE consistently outperforms petr4, sometimes by several orders of magnitude. While HOL4P4.EXE does not yet match the performance of the reference software switch BMv2, implemented in C++, it shows that the formal guarantees can be achieved without sacrificing real-world usability.

4.1   Extraction and Compilation Measurements

The verified code extraction of the semantics and the V1Model architecture model takes 10 m, while extraction of the `vss-example.p4` program takes 4m35s with no additional table entries and 5 m with 100 additional entries. Note that the extraction of table entries can be separated from that of the program, so that re-compiling the same switch with new table entries can be done in seconds. The code extraction of `port_swap.p4` takes 3m25s and that of `fabric_border_router.p4` 6 m. The final step of compilation to binary only takes a few seconds.

The BMv2 binary is 2.5 MB and the petr4 binary is 27.5 MB. For `port_swap.p4`, the HOL4P4.EXE binary is 970 kB, for `vss-example.p4` it is 1.1 MB and for `fabric_border_router.p4` 2.0 MB. Notably, since the program is linked in the binary instead of parsed at run-time (as for petr4 and BMv2), the HOL4P4.EXE size increases with the size of the P4 program that is used, but remains smaller than for the alternatives.

---

[4] The testbed is available in the Github repository https://github.com/kth-step/swswitch-perf at the tag `VSTTE2025`.

[5] Using the Mininet-capable version in the branch `mininet-integration` that was presented at CAV 2021 [6]. Printing of debug messages and related calculations were commented out in the source code to increase performance.

4.2 Zero-Load UDP Latency

The zero-load latency of different P4-programmable software switch solutions
running `port_swap.p4` is shown in Fig. 3a

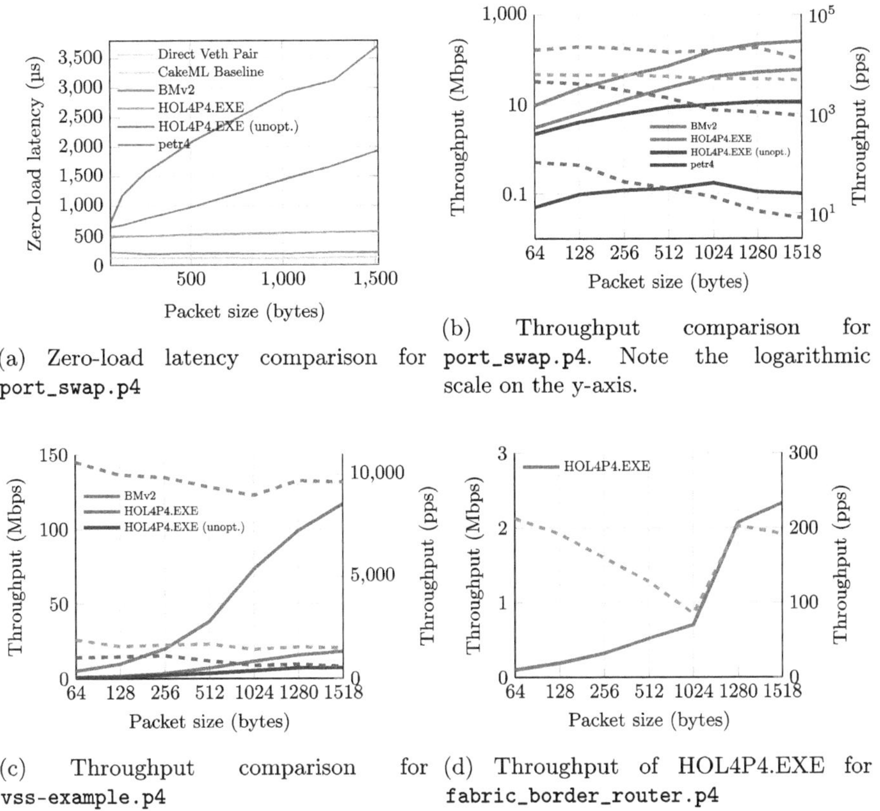

(a) Zero-load latency comparison for
`port_swap.p4`

(b) Throughput comparison for
`port_swap.p4`. Note the logarithmic
scale on the y-axis.

(c) Throughput comparison for
`vss-example.p4`

(d) Throughput of HOL4P4.EXE for
`fabric_border_router.p4`

Fig. 3. Performance measurements. Solid and dashed lines are scaled according to the
left and right y-axes, respectively.

Among the software switches, BMv2 achieves a roughly constant latency of
200 µs regardless of packet size, whereas both petr4 and HOL4P4.EXE have a linearly increasing latency, with HOL4P4.EXE almost achieving constant latency.
The performance of petr4 seems to slowly degrade the longer the switch is running, implying issues with garbage collection. The cost of the HOL4P4.EXE
semantics interpreting `port_swap.p4` is roughly 520 µs, which is obtained by sub-
tracting the latency of the CakeML baseline solution from that of HOL4P4.EXE.

The conclusions from measuring zero-load latency for `vss-example.p4` are
similar to those from the `port_swap.p4` case, with BMv2 and HOL4P4.EXE
achieving a near-constant 360 and 1400 µs, respectively, and petr4 scaling from

around 2400 to 14000 µs. The large `fabric_border_router.p4` program incurs a larger latency of 16.5 ms when using HOL4P4.EXE.

We performed throughput testing using an RFC2544-derived method. The results for `port_swap.p4` are shown in Fig. 3b

The throughput results of the VSS example, shown in Fig. 3c

4.3   Table Usage

In order to benchmark performance over different table sizes, the `vss-example.p4` program was used with different numbers of random, non-matching, non-overlapping entries (32-bit IPv4 addresses) inserted before the matching entries in an existing table. The packet size for this test was 1518 bytes. BMv2 manages to keep latency roughly constant, while each additional table entry contributes around 3 µs for HOL4P4.EXE and 1.6 µs for petr4.

5   Conclusions and Future Work

We have presented HOL4P4.EXE, the first P4 software switch built with formal correctness guarantees, and demonstrated that it outperforms a previous semantics-based solution by orders of magnitude and fulfils minimum requirements for practical use. In summary, efficient prototype trusted execution can be achieved via verified compilation of an executable semantics, especially when optimizations are in place.

A complete formal proof that the entire optimized version of the HOL4P4 semantics preserves the original semantics under transformation to the optimized state is currently in progress. However, the new semantics of arithmetic using bitstrings has been proved to completely implement the old word-based solution, and all adjustments to the standard executable semantics have been proved to keep the soundness with respect to the relational semantics. All versions of the executable semantics have been successfully validated against the standard test suite used for HOL4P4.

A future task could be to prove the CakeML wrapper functionally correct by using the existing characteristic formulae-based tools for CakeML [2,7].

Our experimental results in Fig. 3ashow promise that future CakeML-based verified compilation techniques that do not rely on compiling an interpreter could outperform BMv2. Firstly, the virtual loop-freeness of P4 programs means one could take the result of symbolic execution [14] and use it to define a function in HOL4 with the symbolic input as parameter, which is then extracted to CakeML (the "CakeML baseline" graph in Fig. 3ais from an unverified version of this approach). Secondly, one could use the HOL4P4 semantics to write a verified compiler to another language, for which there already exists a verified compiler: ideal candidates for this are the low-level systems language Pancake [20] or Verilog [12,13]. However, this approach might require a larger proof effort.

Acknowledgments. This work was in part financially supported by Digital Futures, and in part by the SEMLA project financed by Vinnova (Sweden's Innovation Agency). We would also like to thank Magnus Myreen for valuable correspondence regarding the usage of CakeML.

References

1. Alshnakat, A., Lundberg, D., Guanciale, R., Dam, M.: HOL4P4: mechanized small-step semantics for P4. Proc. ACM Program. Lang. **8**(OOPSLA1), 223–249 (2024). https://doi.org/10.1145/3649819
2. Åman Pohjola, J., Rostedt, H., Myreen, M.O.: Characteristic formulae for liveness properties of non-terminating CakeML programs. In: 10th International Conference on Interactive Theorem Proving (ITP 2019), pp. 1–19 (2019). https://doi.org/10.4230/LIPIcs.ITP.2019.32
3. Chavanon, C., Besson, F., Ninet, T.: PfComp: a verified compiler for packet filtering leveraging binary decision diagrams. In: Proceedings of the 13th ACM SIGPLAN International Conference on Certified Programs and Proofs, pp. 89–102. CPP 2024 (2024). https://doi.org/10.1145/3636501.3636954
4. Doenges, R., et al.: Petr4: formal foundations for p4 data planes. Proc. ACM Program. Lang. **5**(POPL) (2021). https://doi.org/10.1145/3434322
5. Doenges, R., Kappé, T., Sarracino, J., Foster, N., Morrisett, G.: Leapfrog: certified equivalence for protocol parsers. In: Proceedings of the 43rd ACM SIGPLAN International Conference on Programming Language Design and Implementation, pp. 950–965. PLDI 2022 (2022). https://doi.org/10.1145/3519939.3523715
6. Foster, N., Tahmasbi Arashloo, M., Parkinson, S.: CAV'21 P4 verification tutorial (2021). https://github.com/cornell-netlab/cav21-tutorial
7. Guéneau, A., Myreen, M.O., Kumar, R., Norrish, M.: Verified characteristic formulae for CakeML. In: Programming Languages and Systems, pp. 584–610 (2017). https://doi.org/10.1007/978-3-662-54434-1_22
8. Intel Corporation: $P4_{16}$ Intel® Tofino™ native architecture - public version (2021). https://github.com/barefootnetworks/Open-Tofino/blob/master/PUBLIC_Tofino-Native-Arch.pdf
9. Kumar, R., Myreen, M.O., Norrish, M., Owens, S.: CakeML: a verified implementation of ML. SIGPLAN Not. **49**(1), 179–191 (2014). https://doi.org/10.1145/2578855.2535841
10. Leroy, X., Blazy, S., Kästner, D., Schommer, B., Pister, M., Ferdinand, C.: CompCert - a formally verified optimizing compiler. In: ERTS 2016: Embedded Real Time Software and Systems, 8th European Congress (2016). https://inria.hal.science/hal-01238879
11. Liu, J., et al.: p4v: practical verification for programmable data planes. In: Proceedings of the 2018 Conference of the ACM Special Interest Group on Data Communication, pp. 490–503. SIGCOMM '18 (2018). https://doi.org/10.1145/3230543.3230582
12. Lööw, A.: Lutsig: a verified Verilog compiler for verified circuit development. In: Proceedings of the 10th ACM SIGPLAN International Conference on Certified Programs and Proofs, pp. 46–60. CPP 2021 (2021). https://doi.org/10.1145/3437992.3439916

13. Lööw, A., Myreen, M.O.: A proof-producing translator for Verilog development in HOL. In: 2019 IEEE/ACM 7th International Conference on Formal Methods in Software Engineering (FormaliSE), pp. 99–108 (2019). https://doi.org/10.1109/FormaliSE.2019.00020
14. Lundberg, D., Guanciale, R., Dam, M.: Proof-producing symbolic execution for P4. In: Verified Software. Theories, Tools and Experiments, pp. 70–83 (2025). https://doi.org/10.1007/978-3-031-86695-1_5
15. Myreen, M.O., Owens, S.: Proof-producing synthesis of ML from higher-order logic. In: Proceedings of the 17th ACM SIGPLAN International Conference on Functional Programming, pp. 115–126. ICFP '12 (2012). https://doi.org/10.1145/2364527.2364545
16. Netflix, Inc.: Netflix-recommended internet speeds (2025). https://help.netflix.com/en/node/306
17. Nötzli, A., Khan, J., Fingerhut, A., Barrett, C., Athanas, P.: P4pktgen: automated test case generation for P4 programs. In: Proceedings of the Symposium on SDN Research, pp. 1–7 (2018). https://doi.org/10.1145/3185467.3185497
18. P4 Language Consortium: behavioral model (BMV2) (2025). https://github.com/p4lang/behavioral-model
19. Peterson, R., et al.: P4Cub: a little language for big routers. In: Proceedings of the 12th ACM SIGPLAN International Conference on Certified Programs and Proofs, pp. 303–319 (2023). https://doi.org/10.1145/3573105.3575670
20. Åman Pohjola, J., et al.: Pancake: verified systems programming made sweeter. In: Proceedings of the 12th Workshop on Programming Languages and Operating Systems, pp. 1–9. PLOS '23 (2023). https://doi.org/10.1145/3623759.3624544
21. Shahbaz, M., Choi, S., Pfaff, B., Kim, C., Feamster, N., McKeown, N., Rexford, J.: Pisces: a programmable, protocol-independent software switch. In: Proceedings of the 2016 ACM SIGCOMM Conference, pp. 525–538. SIGCOMM '16 (2016). https://doi.org/10.1145/2934872.2934886
22. SONiC Foundation: PINS infrastructure (2025). https://github.com/sonic-net/sonic-pins
23. Stoenescu, R., Dumitrescu, D., Popovici, M., Negreanu, L., Raiciu, C.: Debugging P4 programs with Vera. In: Proceedings of the 2018 Conference of the ACM Special Interest Group on Data Communication, pp. 518–532 (2018). https://doi.org/10.1145/3230543.3230548
24. Tan, Y.K., Myreen, M.O., Kumar, R., Fox, A., Owens, S., Norrish, M.: The verified CakeML compiler backend. J. Functional Program. **29** (2019). https://doi.org/10.1017/S0956796818000229
25. The P4 Language Consortium: P4$_{16}$ language specification (2024). https://p4.org/wp-content/uploads/sites/53/2024/10/P4-16-spec-v1.2.5.html
26. Wang, Q., Pan, M., Wang, S., Doenges, R., Beringer, L., Appel, A.W.: Foundational verification of stateful P4 packet processing. In: 14th International Conference on Interactive Theorem Proving (ITP 2023). Schloss-Dagstuhl-Leibniz Zentrum für Informatik (2023). https://doi.org/10.4230/LIPIcs.ITP.2023.32
27. Wang, S., Pan, M., Appel, A.W.: Comprehensive verification of packet processing (2024). https://doi.org/10.48550/arXiv.2412.19908
28. Wiles, K.: Pktgen - traffic generator powered by DPDK (2025). https://github.com/pktgen/Pktgen-DPDK
29. Zoom Communications, Inc.: Zoom system requirements: windows, macOS, Linux (2025). https://support.zoom.com/hc/en/article?id=zm_kb&sysparm_article=KB0060748

Bounding the Execution Cost of WebAssembly Functions

John Shortt[1]([✉]) [iD], Amy Felty[1] [iD], and Anil Somayaji[2] [iD]

[1] University of Ottawa, Ottawa, ON, Canada
{jshor018,afelty}@uottawa.ca
[2] Carleton University, Ottawa, ON, Canada
soma@scs.carleton.ca

Abstract. Bounds on worst-case execution time can improve system reliability and security in a variety of contexts. Past work on bounding execution time has faced challenges due to the lack of formal specifications of mainstream computing environments. WebAssembly (Wasm) is a low-level language originally designed for efficient execution in browsers that is used today in edge computing and other environments. Wasm has been formally specified and has a mechanized soundness proof, greatly facilitating the formal analysis of Wasm programs. Here, we present a new tool for bounding the worst-case execution time of WebAssembly functions that is based on the formalization of Wasm. We have tested our tool on significantly more and larger functions than those studied in previous work (over 107,000 functions, with the longest function being 4156 lines of Wasm from 392 lines of C), and it successfully and efficiently analyzed the vast majority of functions tested. Progress in our tool suggests the feasibility of calculating worst-case execution bounds on large real-world code bases.

Keywords: Program Analysis · Execution Cost Analysis · Formal Verification · WebAssembly

1 Introduction

In the context of web applications, edge computing, digital contracts, and numerous rich document formats, systems execute untrusted code. If not properly contained, such code can consume arbitrary resources, resulting in denials of service, battery exhaustion, information theft, and application and host compromises. Language and operating system sandboxes can limit the potential damage of malicious code, but to accommodate increasingly complex applications, such sandboxes must allow code to have significant CPU and memory resources. Fixed limits can reduce, but not eliminate, the risk of giving arbitrary code access to CPU and memory resources. Worst-case execution time (WCET), however, offers an alternative defense strategy: By calculating the worst-case execution time of a program in advance, it becomes possible to decide not to run code if it will

C. Pit-Claudel and K. Kosaian (Eds.): VSTTE 2025, LNCS 16499, pp. 83–100, 2026.
https://doi.org/10.1007/978-3-032-27340-6_6

consume too many resources. As we know, this problem cannot be solved in the general case (otherwise we would have a solution to the halting problem [21]), but we also know that formally defined systems can be reasoned about with sophisticated tools that allow us to draw interesting conclusions about the behavior of those systems.

Today WebAssembly (Wasm) [17,25] is the leading technology for untrusted code written in arbitrary programming languages. Wasm is widely deployed in web browsers, is an enabling technology for edge computing, and is finding applications in other domains. Two properties in particular contribute to offering a path toward bounding the execution time of programs: it is low level, and it is formally specified. With regard to the first property, Wasm can serve as a compilation target much like CPU-specific assembly languages and bytecode languages such as the Java Virtual Machine (JVM) and Common Language Runtime (CLR). Wasm's appeal comes from highly sand-boxed yet very efficient runtimes, something that is not generally available for other compiler targets. The second key property, the fact that Wasm has been formally specified, greatly facilitates program analysis. The formal specification ensures that Wasm does not have undefined behavior, and its program control flow mechanisms use the ideas of structured programming in a way that also simplifies the reasoning about them. Other compiler targets have been formalized; however, these formalizations are post hoc and often only approximate the functioning of the language in practice. In contrast, Wasm has been formally specified from the beginning, thus making it an important application area for program analysis techniques both because of potential practical applications and because it has been designed to facilitate formal program analysis.

Our tool, which we call **Wanalyze**, and is available on GitHub[1], shows the potential of Wasm to simplify formal program analysis, for example by eliminating the need to detect loops (they are evident in the structured control flow) and reducing the need for directly analyzing complex data structures (WebAssembly has few data types and simple data structures), while still allowing large-scale production code to be analyzed. Further, because Wasm itself is formally specified, our results apply not to idealized execution environments (as is often the case for C variants), but to production runtimes.

As a step towards this goal, we have chosen to focus on analyzing individual functions rather than entire programs. Specifically, the scope of our work is the static analysis of each function in a Wasm module to determine a bound on its cost of execution. As we discuss later, previous work in the literature shows how this can be extended to whole programs [2–4,6]. Although we do not fully handle whole programs, we are able to analyze functions that are much larger than the programs analyzed in previous work (up to four times larger) and for over 107,000 functions from real-world code bases, giving us a breadth of experience significantly beyond that of past work.

In this paper, we present the methods we have developed for calculating the worst-case cost of Wasm functions and our efforts to validate our methods.

---

[1] https://www.github.com/jsCarleton/wanalyze.

Wanalyze is implemented in OCaml, consists of approximately 5000 lines of code, is licensed under the Apache 2.0 license, and is available for download. We have evaluated **Wanalyze** on Wasm programs and libraries of varying complexity and have found that it is able to successfully produce execution bounds for the vast majority of these functions, while being able to analyze thousands of lines of code per second in our tests run on relatively modest hardware.

The contributions of this paper consist of the following: the software tool, **Wanalyze**, which is the first published application that can bound the worst-case cost of WebAssembly functions, demonstrating the feasibility of bounding real-world code with the analysis of over 107,000 functions.

In the rest of this paper, Sect. 2 contains a motivating example for the techniques that we use. Section 3 contains details of our analysis techniques. In Sect. 4 we describe the experimental tests that have been performed and their results. We discuss related work in Sect. 5. Section 6 concludes.

2   Example

By way of example, we examine the Wasm code for the inner loop of a bubble sort implementation. Listing 1 contains a C implementation, and Listing 2 contains the skeleton of the Wasm code to which this C code compiles. The latter shows the branching structure of the Wasm code and is annotated with comments that define the blocks of code in that structure. It also includes annotations (labels) that define the instructions that can be branched to and the destination of a branching instruction.

```
 1    void bubble(int n, int* data) {
 2      int i, j, temp;
 3
 4      for(i = 0; i < n - 1; i++) {
 5        for(j = 0; j < n - i - 1; j++) {
 6          if(data[j] > data[j + 1]) {
 7              temp = data[j];
 8              data[j] = data[j + 1];
 9              data[j + 1] = temp;
10          }
11        }
12      }
13    }
```

Listing 1. C code to implement bubble sort

```
 1        (func (;6;) (type 6) (param i32 i32)
 2          (local i32 i32 i32 i32 i32 i32 i32 i32)
 3          ;; BB 0
 4         block   ;;label = @1
 5          ;; BB 1 (deleted 3 lines)
 9            br_if 0 (;@1;)
10            ;; BB 2 (deleted 7 lines)
18            loop   ;;label = @2
19              ;; BB 3 (deleted 2 lines)
22              block   ;;label = @3
23                ;; BB 4 (deleted 7 lines)
31                br_if 0 ;;label = @3
32                ;; BB 5
33                loop   ;;label = @4
34                  ;; BB 6
35                  block   ;;label = @5
36                  ;; BB 7
37                    ;; (deleted 20 lines)
57                    br_if 0 ;;label = @5
58                    ;; BB 8 (deleted 6 lines)
65                  end
66                  ;; BB 9 (deleted 3 lines)
70                  br_if 0 ;;label = @4
71                  ;; BB 10
72                end
73                ;; BB 11
74              end
75              ;; BB 12 (deleted 10 lines)
86              br_if 0 ;;label = @2
87              ;; BB 13
88            end
89            ;; BB 14
90          end
91          ;; BB 15
92        )
```

Listing 2. Outline of Wasm code to implement bubble sort

Figure 1 shows the branching structure of Listing 2 in the form of a control flow diagram. In this diagram, nodes represent *basic blocks* (BBs) and edges are possible execution paths. Red-dashed edges represent backward execution paths to the beginning of a loop. Figure 2 shows how we can further refine this block structure by merging consecutive blocks when there is only one code path through them. In doing so, we retain information about the flow of control in the function and create a higher level control flow diagram with fewer nodes. In this diagram, nodes represent *super blocks* (SBs) and, again, edges are possible

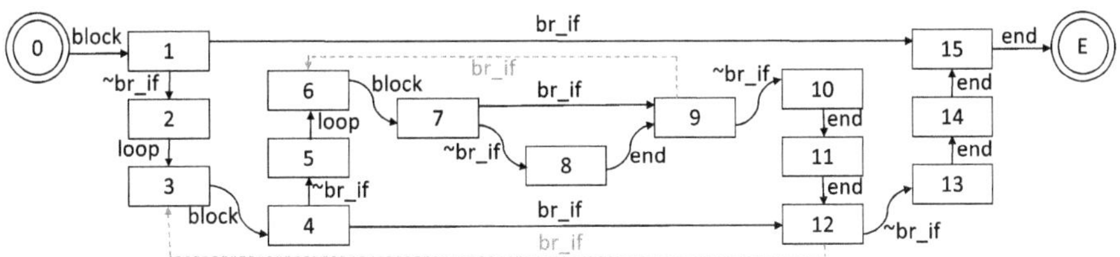

Fig. 1. Basic block control flow diagram for bubble sort

execution paths. There are two types of superblock: those that do not contain a loop, shown as a rectangle with a black border, and those that do, shown with a red dotted border. The term basic block comes from the compiler and static analysis literature [13,14]. We define these block types precisely for Wasm in the next section.

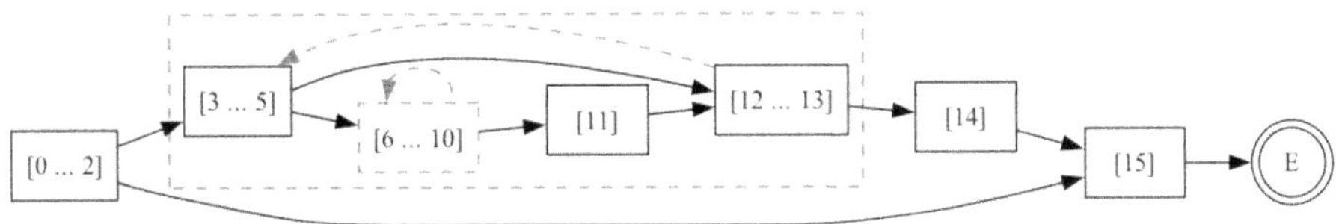

Fig. 2. Super block control flow diagram for bubble sort

Lines 37 through 70 of Listing 2 contain the code that implements the body of the inner-most loop of bubble sort. Lines of code are removed from the listing for presentation purposes. Table 1, column (b) contains all of this code, including the missing lines from the listing, with line numbers in column (a). In this table n[i] and m[i] refer to local variables and memory locations i, respectively. Column (c) is the contents of the Wasm value stack after the instruction is executed and any changes to variables or memory that the instruction causes. We use the convention that the left-most item in the stack is the one most recently added. Lines with comments in the listing are omitted from the table. To improve readability, we also convert the label indices in the branch instructions to line numbers. For this table, it is sufficient to know that n is an array containing function parameters and local variables, and m is an array representing Wasm memory.

In summary, this code behaves as follows: in lines 37 through 49 the 2 values to be compared are loaded into temporary variables, and the loop counter is updated (line 49), in lines 50 through 65 the two values are swapped if they are not in the correct order, and in lines 67 through 70 the loop counter is compared to the loop bound to determine if another loop pass is required. The variable n[5] is used for the loop counter and is modified only on line 49. The variable n[4] is used as the loop bound and is not modified in the loop body. Note that the code fragment uses variables like n[4] that have been previously initialized.

Table 1. Symbolic execution of bubble sort inner loop and SSA form

(a) Line	(b) Instruction	(c) Updated stack contents/Instruction side effects	(d) Equivalent SSA
37	`local.get 1`	`[n[1]]`	$t_1 \leftarrow n[1]$
38	`local.get 5`	`[n[5]; n[1]]`	$t_2 \leftarrow n[5]$
39	`i32.const 2`	`[2; n[5]; n[1]]`	$t_3 \leftarrow 2$
40	`i32.shl`	`[(n[5] shl 2); n[1]]`	$t_4 \leftarrow t_2 \ shl \ t_3$
41	`i32.add`	`[n[1] + (n[5] shl 2)]`	$t_5 \leftarrow t_4 + t_1$
42	`local.tee 6`	`[n[1] + (n[5] shl 2)]`	$n[6] \leftarrow t_5$
		`n[6] ← n[1] + (n[5] shl 2)`	
43	`i32.load`	`[m[n[1] + (n[5] shl 2)]]`	$t_6 \leftarrow m[t_5]$
44	`local.tee 7`	`[m[n[1] + (n[5] shl 2)]]`	$n[7] \leftarrow t_6$
		`n[7] ← m[n[1] + (n[5] shl 2)]`	
45	`local.get 1`	`[n[1]; m[n[1] + (n[5] shl 2)]]`	$t_7 \leftarrow n[1]$
46	`local.get 5`	`[n[5]; n[1]; m[n[1] + (n[5] shl 2)]]`	$t_8 \leftarrow n[5]$
47	`i32.const 1`	`[1; n[5]; n[1]; m[n[1] + (n[5] shl 2)]]`	$t_9 \leftarrow 1$
48	`i32.add`	`[n[5] + 1; n[1]; m[n[1] + (n[5] shl 2)]]`	$t_{10} \leftarrow t_8 + t_9$
49	`local.tee 5`	`[n[5] + 1; n[1]; m[n[1] + (n[5] shl 2)]]`	$n[5] \leftarrow t_{10}$
		`n[5] ← n[5] + 1`	
50	`i32.const 2`	`[2; n[5] + 1; n[1];` `m[n[1] + (n[5] shl 2)]]`	$t_{11} \leftarrow 2$
51	`i32.shl`	`[((n[5] + 1) shl 2); n[1];` `m[n[1] + (n[5] shl 2)]]`	$t_{12} \leftarrow t_{10} \ shl \ t_{11}$
52	`i32.add`	`[n[1] + ((n[5] + 1) shl 2);` `m[n[1] + (n[5] shl 2)]]`	$t_{13} \leftarrow t_{11} + t_{12}$
53	`local.tee 8`	`[n[1] + ((n[5] + 1) shl 2);` `m[n[1] + (n[5] shl 2)]]`	$n[8] \leftarrow t_{13}$
		`n[8] ← n[1] + ((n[5] + 1) shl 2)`	
54	`i32.load`	`[m[n[1] + ((n[5] + 1) shl 2)];` `m[n[1] + (n[5] shl 2)]]`	$t_{14} \leftarrow m[t_{13}]$
55	`local.tee 9`	`[m[n[1] + ((n[5] + 1) shl 2)];` `m[n[1] + (n[5] shl 2)]]`	$n[9] \leftarrow t_{14}$
		`n[9] ← m[((n[5] + 1) shl 2) + n[1]]`	
56	`i32.le_s`	`[m[n[1] + (n[5] shl 2)] ≤` `m[n[1] + ((n[5] + 1) shl 2)]]`	$t_{15} \leftarrow t_{14} \leq t_6$
57	`br_if 67`	`[]`	t_{15}
59	`local.get 6`	`[n[6]]`	$t_{16} \leftarrow n[6]$
60	`local.get 9`	`[n[9]; n[6]]`	$t_{17} \leftarrow n[9]$
61	`i32.store`	`[]`	$m[t_{17}] \leftarrow t_{16}$
		`m[n[9]] ← n[6]`	
62	`local.get 8`	`[n[8]]`	$t_{18} \leftarrow n[8]$
63	`local.get 7`	`[n[7]; n[8]]`	$t_{19} \leftarrow n[7]$
64	`i32.store`	`[]`	$m[t_{19}] \leftarrow t_{18}$
		`m[n[7]] ← n[8]`	
65	`end`	`[]`	
67	`local.get 5`	`[n[5]]`	$t_{20} \leftarrow n[5]$
68	`local.get 4`	`[n[4]; n[5]]`	$t_{21} \leftarrow n[4]$
69	`i32.ne`	`[n[5] ≠ n[4]]`	$t_{22} \leftarrow t_{21} \neq t_{20}$
70	`br_if 37`	`[]`	t_{22}

We use symbolic execution and single-assignment form (SSA) [16] to determine
the value of these variables when the loop is entered.

Column (c) of Table 1 can be created by symbolically executing the corresponding Wasm code. Symbolic execution is a method of recording the effects on the machine state symbolically, instruction by instruction, when executing a code fragment. It gives us the ability to inspect the state of the virtual machine at any point in a function's execution. For example, we can look at a basic block that ends with a conditional branch instruction and determine symbolically on what expression the conditional branch is based. Symbols shown in column (c) represent the values of the respective variables when they are placed on the stack, not subsequently updated values.

Column (d) is an expression of the effect of the corresponding instruction (from column (b)). It is in SSA form.

We can observe the following facts about the code in the table for the inner loop of bubble sort:

- The loop tests the condition $n[5] \neq n[4]$ on line 69 (we can see this on the value stack) and continues execution via the `br_if` instruction on line 70 if this condition is true. Thus, the variables that determine when this loop ends are $n[4]$ and $n[5]$.
- From the side effects of the instruction in column (c), we see that the variable $n[4]$ is not modified.
- Similarly, we see that the variable $n[5]$ is modified on line 49 (only), where it is incremented.

From these observations, we can see that the number of times this loop body will be executed is determined by the values of $n[4]$ and $n[5]$ when the loop body is entered. In the next section, we describe how we use this information to determine a bound on the number of loop iterations, and we elaborate on how this information can be used to determine a bound on execution cost.

3   Approach

In this section we describe our approach to producing bounds on Wasm functions. The **Wanalyze** tool reads a Wasm binary module as its input and analyzes each of the functions contained in that module. It outputs an expression, in terms of the function inputs, for an upper bound on the cost of executing the function.

Note that our cost model assumes that all Wasm instructions and all functions called (in either Wasm or native code) take the same amount of time to execute, allowing us to use the executed instruction count within a function as a proxy for code execution time. We count this as one unit of execution cost. Although this simplification precludes precise execution bounds, such bounds are not feasible with Wasm in general, because of it being an execution format designed for portable, optimizing language runtimes; however, as we show in Sect. 4, this simplified model is sufficient to calculate consistent execution bounds.

Algorithm 1. Get SBs from BBs

```
 1: function SBsOfBBs(BBs, SBs, SB, loop_nesting)
 2:     while BBs ≠ [] do
 3:         BB ← car(BBs)
 4:         BBs ← cdr(BBs)
 5:         // are we beginning a loop?
 6:         if BB.type = LOOP then
 7:             // yes, close off the current SB, if any, and start a new one
 8:             if SB ≠ [] then
 9:                 SBs ← SBs + SB
10:             end if
11:             return SBsOfBBs(BBs, SBs, [BB], loop_nesting + 1)
12:         else
13:             // are we ending a loop?
14:             if BB.type = END and BB.nesting = loop_nesting then
15:                 // yes, close off the SB and start a new SB
16:                 SBs ← SBs + (SB + BB)
17:                 SB.children ← SBsOFBBs(SB, [], [], loop_nesting)
18:                 SB ← []
19:                 loop_nesting ← loop_nesting − 1
20:             else
21:                 // Does this BB have predecessors not in the current SB?
22:                 if BB.predecessors \ SB ≠ [] then
23:                     // Yes, start a new SB
24:                     return SBsOfBBs(BBs, SBs + SB, [BB], loop_nesting)
25:                 else
26:                     // No need to start a new SB
27:                     SB ← SB + BB
28:                 end if
29:             end if
30:         end if
31:     end while
32:     // close off the current SB, if any
33:     if SB ≠ [] then
34:         SBs ← SBs + SB
35:     end if
36:     return SBs
37: end function
```

Basic Blocks. We first generate a set of basic blocks [14] for each function based on the following definition:

Definition 1. *(Basic Blocks of a Wasm function) The (set of) Basic Blocks (BBs) of a Wasm function are consecutive lines of code with the following properties:*

- *each instruction in the body of the function is contained in exactly one BB,*

- *each BB ends with a* `block, loop, if, else, end, br, br_if, br_table, return, unreachable` *instruction and contains no other occurrences of any of these instructions.*

Because a BB contains no conditional execution paths, its cost can be determined precisely as the number of instructions in the BB.

Super Blocks. Aggregating BBs into Super Blocks (SBs) as we did in Fig. 2 allows us to analyze loop structures more readily. In our definition, an SB is composed of consecutive BBs, and, in the case of nested loops, other SBs.

Definition 2. *(Super Block of a Wasm function) The conditions that determine how BBs are assigned to SBs are as follows:*

- <u>C1</u> *There is an SB for each* `loop/end` *structure block in the function. It contains the BBs of that code fragment beginning with the first BB after the* `loop` *instruction and ending with, and including, the BB containing the associated* **end** *instruction.*
- <u>C2</u> *A function's flow of execution can only enter an SB at the first BB in the SB.*
- <u>C3</u> *Consecutive BBs with no loops appear in the same SB subject to C2.*

Algorithm 1 describes how the list of SBs is determined. In addition to the code, each basic block has some attributes, including its *type* (e.g., *LOOP, END*), its *nesting* level, which indicates the depth of the loop (if any) in which it is contained, and its *predecessors*, which include all previous basic blocks. A single pass is made through the basic blocks that make up the function, emitting super blocks whenever the conditions to create a new one or end the current one are satisfied. These conditions are on lines 6, 14, and 21 of the algorithm. Their meaning is as follows:

- line 6: the first basic block of a loop has been reached,
- line 14: the end basic block of a loop has been reached,
- line 21: a basic block with multiple entry points has been reached.

Code Path Generation. If an SB has no loops we can bound its cost as: *the maximum cost over all paths from the root of the control flow graph to a leaf node* , where we consider the cost of a path to be the sum of the cost of the BBs on that path. That is, we consider all possible execution paths through the SB and take the maximum cost of those execution paths as our upper bound on the SB cost.

In general, we evaluate the cost of each code path to compute a bound on the function cost.

Symbolic Execution and Static Single-Assignment (SSA) Form. Symbolic execution models the effects of code on machine state symbolically, instruction by instruction. It gives us the ability to inspect the state of the virtual machine at any point in a function's execution. Column (c) of Table 1 shows the results of symbolic execution for our example.

We can use symbolic execution to determine the condition under which a loop terminates. To find a bound on the number of loop iterations, we need another technique that allows us to symbolically evaluate the values of the variables in the condition. To do this, we perform *program slicing* [27] on the SSA. Column (d) of Table 1 shows this result for our example.

Approach to Determining Loop Execution Cost. As mentioned, the execution cost of an SB is bounded by the cost of the maximum cost path. There is no general solution to this problem (otherwise we would have a solution to the halting problem, as mentioned earlier). Our approach is based on rules that recognize specific patterns in loop structures.

A loop body is an SB, thus giving us a bound on the execution of a loop body. To arrive at an expression for a bound on a loop, we must determine a bound on the number of iterations. We then combine these two bounds to arrive at an expression for a bound on the loop execution cost, which will generally include the parameters of the function. We need to know the following:

- L1: conditions that cause the loop to exit;
- L2: variables used to evaluate these conditions;
- L3: initial values of these variables when the loop is entered;
- L4: how the variables are updated in the loop.

To determine L1, the tool determines all possible paths through the body of the loop that either exit the loop or return to the top of the loop. The tool then symbolically executes these paths to determine the contents of the value stack when a looping condition is evaluated. Since we want conditions that cause the loop to exit, this looping condition is negated if control returns to the top of the loop. This produces a list of loop conditions, one for each path through the loop body. We can then parse these conditions to determine which variables they use, which gives us L2. From line 69 in the example, we can see that the variables in this case are $n[4]$ and $n[5]$. For each variable, we can then create the SSA form for all function execution paths to the loop SB. We can then simplify these SSA to get the possible values of the variables at the loop entry. This gives us L3. Finally, we can create an SSA form for each of the variables, but this time simplify it over all execution paths from the first BB of the loop to the BB of their associated condition. This will give us L4.

This result is then used to apply a set of rules depending on the condition and the manner in which the condition variables are updated to determine the number of loop iterations. In our tests, we found that a small number of rules, usually based on observing a loop counter representing the size of a data structure or a static loop limit, allowed most loop constructs to be analyzed to produce a bound on the number of iterations. We believe that this is due to the fact that the structured control flow found in the source language (e.g. C or Rust) translates readily into Wasm.

Cost Analysis. We compose the analyses based on bounds on the costs of BBs, SBs, and loops using code path generation, symbolic execution, and SSA to produce a bound on the execution cost of the function. In describing these costs, we use the phrase *SB path* to mean an execution path that is made up of SBs. We say *linear SB path* to mean a path that does not loop. The SBs that make up the path may contain loops, but at the level of the path there are no loops. Similarly, a *BB path* is an execution path that is made up of BBs and a *linear BB path* is a path with no loops. We also introduce some notation:

- We use f to denote a function, X to denote the input to the function, sp for an SB path, both s and sc denote an SB, bp a BB path and b a BB.
- For an SB s, let $S(s)$ be the set of all linear SB paths of SBs in s that start at the first SB of s and exit s. That is, we restrict $S(s)$ to contain only paths that are non-looping and are made up of SBs contained in s. We extend this notation to functions; $S(f)$ denotes all linear SB paths through the function f.
- Let $nS(sp)$ be the set of SBs without a loop that are on the SB path sp.
- Let $lS(sp)$ be the set of SBs with a loop that are on the SB path sp
- For a looping SB s, let $N(s, X)$ be a bound on the number of times the loop will iterate given function inputs X.
- Let $B(s)$ be the set of all linear BB paths of the SB s.
- Let s_f be the SB that contains all of f.

With this notation, we can express the following equalities and inequalities for bounding the cost of a function:

$$cost_F(f, X) \leq \max_{sp \in S(f)} cost_{pS}(sp, X) \tag{1}$$

$$cost_{pS}(sp, X) \leq \sum_{s \in nS(sp)} cost_S(s) + \sum_{s \in lS(sp)} [\max_{sp' \in S(s)} cost_{pS}(sp', X)] * N(s, X) \tag{2}$$

$$cost_S(s) \leq \max_{bp \in B(s)} cost_{pB}(bp) \tag{3}$$

$$cost_{pB}(bp) = \sum_{b \in bp} cost_B(b) \tag{4}$$

$$cost_B(b) = \text{number of instructions in BB } b \tag{5}$$

In these equations, the subscript F is for the cost of the function, pS for the cost of an SB path, S for an SB, pB for a BB path, and B for a BB. The equations can be summarized as follows: (1) the cost of a function is bounded by the maximum of the cost of all SB paths through the function; (2) the cost of an SB path is bounded by the sum of the cost of each non-looping SBs in the path plus, inductively, the cost of each of the looping SBs times the number of loop iterations; (3) the cost of an SB is bounded by the maximum cost of all BB paths of the SB; (4) the cost of a BB path is the sum of the cost of the BBs in the path; and (5) the cost of a BB is the number of instructions in the BB.

Objects in Memory. A case that warrants specific mention is that of objects in memory and functions that operate on those objects. Generally, if a function contains code that loops over an object structure and has a loop termination condition that depends only on that data in the object, then **Wanalyze** will not be able to produce a bound for that function.

4   Test Results

We discuss three experiments that we have carried out, followed by an analysis of the results.

Bubble Sort. The focus of the first experiment was the bubble sort code described in Sect. 2. Thus, we start with a relatively simple test case that contains both a nested loop and conditional execution paths. We chose this example to determine whether **Wanalyze** could successfully produce a prediction of the number of instructions to be executed and to determine how accurate that prediction was compared to actual measurements.

This experiment was run in two parts. The first part involved running the bubble sort Wasm code using the **wasmtime** [11] Wasm runtime. This runtime has the ability to instrument Wasm code to measure the amount of "fuel" the code consumes when executed. Conveniently, it measures fuel as the number of instructions executed with the exception of `nop`, `drop`, `block`, and `loop` instructions.

The bubble sort Wasm function takes as input a fixed length array of 32 bit integers and sorts them in place. It is well known that the performance of bubble sort is dependent on the composition of the data. Worst case performance occurs when the input data are ordered in the complete reverse of the sorted data. We ran two different tests to compare the results. The first test was with the data in this worst-case reverse-sorted order; the second test was done with the data in random order. Ten runs were performed with input arrays sized between 10,000 and 100,000 in increments of 10,000. In order to run this Wasm code with **wasmtime**, it was necessary to write "glue" code in Rust that creates the data. This code loads the Wasm module containing the bubble sort, runs it and reports on the amount of fuel consumed.

The second part of the experiment involved running **Wanalyze** on the WebAssembly bubble sort function. The analysis was successful and produced the following polynomial, which is typical of the general format produced:

$$\frac{1}{2}(31n^2 + 11n - 20)$$

as the bound on the number of instructions that would be executed when sorting n items. This agrees with the well-known fact that bubble sort takes $O(n^2)$ time to execute.

Table 2. Bubble sort bound vs. actual - **wasmtime** fuel

Items (K)	**Wanalyze** Bound (M)	Worst-case Actual (M)	Difference	Random A ctual (M)	Difference
10	1,595	1,550	2.90%	1,401	13.85%
20	6,800	6,200	1.61%	5,601	12.48%
30	14,105	13,950	1.11%	12,594	12.00%
40	25,010	24,800	0.85%	22,401	11.65%
50	39,015	38,750	0.68%	35,000	11.47%
60	56,120	55,800	0.57%	50,397	11.36%
70	76,325	75,950	0.49%	68,625	11.22%
80	99,630	99,200	0.43%	89,597	11.20%
90	126,035	125,550	0.39%	113,400	11.14%
100	155,540	155,000	0.35%	139,990	11.11%

Table 2 contains the results of both parts of the experiment. The column titled "**Wanalyze** Bound" shows the bound that **Wanalyze** produced for the number of instructions (in millions) executed to sort that many items. The next column "Worst-case Actual" is the number of instructions reported by **wasmtime** when sorting a set of items that is initially in the complete reverse of sorted order. The column "Random Actual" is the number of instructions, but this time the set to be sorted is initially in random order. The two percentage columns are the differences between the **Wanalyze** bound and the actual measured result in **wasmtime**.

Dhrystone Benchmark. The second experiment followed a similar procedure as the first, but this time the Wasm code generated by the **emscripten** toolchain for version 2.1 of the Dhrystone benchmark [20] was analyzed. The Dhrystone benchmark performance is expected to be linear in the number of iterations. Inspection of the code verifies that this is the case, and **Wanalyze** produces a cost bound of:

$$1033n + 2578$$

where n is the number of Dhrystone iterations performed. See Table 3 for detailed measurements.

In this case, no glue layer code was necessary because the Dhrystone program has no input data. The number of iterations to be performed is a parameter that is compiled into the program.

The results in Table 3 follow a similar format to those for bubble sort. The difference is that since there is no input data to consider, it was only necessary to run a single test for a given number of iterations.

Table 3. Dhrystone predicted/actual

Iterations	wasmtime	**Wanalyze**		
		Actual	Bound	Difference
12,088	7,834	12,487	59.39%
15,110	9,792	15,609	59.41%
18,666	12,100	19,282	59.36%
20,336	13,180	21,007	59.39%
31,110	20,183	32,137	59.23%

MUSL C Library, AutoCAD Application. The third experiment consisted of running **Wanalyze** on the Wasm code for the MUSL C runtime library [23] and the AutoCAD application [8]. Each of these is a large code base, and so they demonstrate the ability of **Wanalyze** to scale. It was necessary to first compile the MUSL library to Wasm. AutoCAD is available for download as a Wasm module.

The entire MUSL library contains over 58,000 lines of code (LOC) in C which, when compiled, results in over 1.26 million lines of Wasm code contained in over 14,000 distinct functions. With an elapsed time of 53 min, this results in a rate of more than 1000 lines of C code analyzed per minute and a rate of 23,000 lines of Wasm analyzed per minute. **Wanalyze** was able to analyze more than 94% of all functions with failure occurring in cases where the number of paths through the function exceeded the built-in limit of one million paths. This limit is used to limit the running time of the analysis and can be extended.

AutoCAD is an order of magnitude larger than the MUSL C library, when measured by lines of Wasm code or number of functions. Comparatively, the elapsed time required to analyze AutoCAD is nearly linear in those metrics (Table 4).

Table 4. MUSL C library, AutoCAD application

	C LOC	Wasm LOC	# functions	Success rate	Elapsed time
MUSL	58,237	1,267,725	14,329	94.6%	53 min
AutoCAD	–	22,641,000	93,664	99.9%	481 min

Analysis. As demonstrated in the final experiment, the performance of **Wanalyze** scales with larger bodies of code. This scaling is driven by these design choices:

- **Wanalyze** makes a single pass through the Wasm binary.
- The algorithms to produce its primary data structures, BBs and SBs, are linear in the number of instructions.
- The number of BBs and SBs produced for a given function is generally an order of magnitude less than the number of instructions in the function.
- The analysis algorithms, symbolic execution, and SSA generation operate in time that is linear in the number of paths through the function.

With both bubble sort and Dhrystone, the bound produced by **Wanalyze** is indeed a bound in that it is greater than the actual measured value. Also, for both, the difference measured is a similar percentage for tests with the same input data. However, this percentage varies between different tests and input data.

These results meet the objective for bounds to be considered reasonable that we set out in the introduction. Execution costs do not exceed the bound, and the bound has the same computational complexity as the function being analyzed. However, we must ask why does the **Wanalyze** bound differ from the actual observed instruction counts? And why does this difference vary between applications and data sets? For example, bubble sort with random data has a difference of 14% (rounded), but Dhrystone has a difference of 59%.

The primary reason for these differences is that **Wanalyze** necessarily chooses the most costly path when evaluating alternative costs in a super block or basic block. In practice, this is a conservative approach because it will often be the case that a less costly path is taken. This means that the accuracy of **Wanalyze**'s bound will depend on how often the costliest path is taken.

This is also an explanation for the differences between applications. Not only do the applications that have lower cost paths that contribute to the **Wanalyze** estimate being higher, but there are differences in the path structure of the functions in the applications. In particular, there is a big difference between the super block control flow diagrams for two functions. Thus, the impact of lower-cost paths will be different between the applications.

The same reasoning also explains why applications that run on different data will have different results. The effect of the lower cost paths will be different when different input data is used.

5   Related Work

The problem of automatically bounding or estimating the cost of execution of a program using static analysis methods has been well studied, starting with the work of Wegbreit [26]. In a series of papers [2,3,6], Albert et al. described their work to solve this problem for Java bytecode. Wegbreit's basic method of analysis is used, but aspects of Java bytecode created additional challenges such as loop detection. A notable contribution of these papers is a theoretical framework for formulating and solving the recurrence relations that are produced by the analysis. Determining a bound on the cost of executing a loop is a core challenge; lexicographic ranking functions [1,2,10] are widely used both to prove loop termination and to determine loop costs.

Some authors [7,19,22,24] focus on the problem of determining the algorithmic complexity of a function and choose to test their solution against well-known algorithms with well-known complexity. Solutions also include consideration of amortized algorithmic costs, which can improve precision. The example given in [19] that demonstrates this benefit is the functional queue, which performs dequeue operations in constant amortized time. The language used in that paper is OCaml. Other languages, such as Raml (resource aware ML) [18], and Solidity (a language for Ethereum smart contracts) [5] have also been studied.

Work in the WCET domain [9,15] has focused on loop analysis. We demonstrate that aspects of Wasm simplify this problem to some extent.

Almost all of the papers mentioned performed experiments using specific data sets consisting of code that was analyzed. Our general observation is that, like the functions in the real-world applications that we analyzed, the test cases consist of a small number of small to medium sized functions or programs. The examples tested in [12] represent a particularly challenging set of loop constructs that are atypical of loop constructs we saw when analyzing real world programs. In contrast, we have taken an empirical approach of analyzing well-known functions, particularly those in an implementation of the standard C library implementation MUSL.

6   Conclusion

As we have shown, Wasm provides a new opportunity to revisit the problem of bounding the execution cost of a program. In particular, it has features that simplify cost analysis, such as structured control flow, which means that it is not necessary to perform loop detection on the input program and translate it to an intermediate structured form. In addition, Wasm only has scalar data types. As a consequence, expensive size analysis methods described in the literature can be greatly simplified.

As future work, we can extend our results to determine a bound on the cost of a whole program, which includes functions that call other functions in the module as well as imported functions, assuming that the Wasm hosting environment will provide the cost of those functions if required. The cost bound of a non-recursive function call will be an expression based on that function's input, which will, in turn, be expressed in terms of the inputs to the calling function. For both recursive and non-recursive calls, we can derive a set of recurrence relations between the costs of these functions. The work by Albert et al. [2–4,6] describes how these recurrence relations can be solved. Future work also includes correctness proofs of our results, which would provide greater assurances in our methods. A mechanization of such a proof would also allow us to add proofs of performance bounds to analyzed functions.

References

1. Albert, E., Arenas, P., Genaim, S., Puebla, G.: Automatic inference of upper bounds for recurrence relations in cost analysis. In: Alpuente, M., Vidal, G. (eds.) SAS 2008. LNCS, vol. 5079, pp. 221–237. Springer, Heidelberg (2008). https://doi.org/10.1007/978-3-540-69166-2_15
2. Albert, E., Arenas, P., Genaim, S., Puebla, G.: Closed-form upper bounds in static cost analysis. J. Autom. Reason. **46**, 161–203 (2011)
3. Albert, E., Arenas, P., Genaim, S., Puebla, G., Zanardini, D.: COSTA: design and implementation of a cost and termination analyzer for java bytecode. In: de Boer, F.S., Bonsangue, M.M., Graf, S., de Roever, W.-P. (eds.) FMCO 2007. LNCS, vol. 5382, pp. 113–132. Springer, Heidelberg (2008). https://doi.org/10.1007/978-3-540-92188-2_5
4. Albert, E., Arenas, P., Genaim, S., Puebla, G., Zanardini, D.: Cost analysis of object-oriented bytecode programs. Theor. Comput. Sci. **413**(1), 142–159 (2012)
5. Albert, E., Correas, J., Gordillo, P., Román-Díez, G., Rubio, A.: Don't run on fumes–parametric gas bounds for smart contracts. J. Syst. Softw. **176**, 110923 (2021)
6. Albert, E., Genaim, S., Masud, A.N.: More precise yet widely applicable cost analysis. In: Jhala, R., Schmidt, D. (eds.) VMCAI 2011. LNCS, vol. 6538, pp. 38–53. Springer, Heidelberg (2011). https://doi.org/10.1007/978-3-642-18275-4_5
7. Alias, C., Darte, A., Feautrier, P., Gonnord, L.: Multi-dimensional rankings, program termination, and complexity bounds of flowchart programs. In: Cousot, R., Martel, M. (eds.) SAS 2010. LNCS, vol. 6337, pp. 117–133. Springer, Heidelberg (2010). https://doi.org/10.1007/978-3-642-15769-1_8
8. AutoCAD: Roundup: The AutoCAD Web App at Google I/O 2018 (2018). https://blogs.autodesk.com/autocad/autocad-web-app-google-io-2018/. Accessed Dec 2022
9. Blazy, S., Maroneze, A., Pichardie, D.: Formal verification of loop bound estimation for WCET analysis. In: Cohen, E., Rybalchenko, A. (eds.) VSTTE 2013. LNCS, vol. 8164, pp. 281–303. Springer, Heidelberg (2014). https://doi.org/10.1007/978-3-642-54108-7_15
10. Bradley, A.R., Manna, Z., Sipma, H.B.: Linear ranking with reachability. In: Etessami, K., Rajamani, S.K. (eds.) CAV 2005. LNCS, vol. 3576, pp. 491–504. Springer, Heidelberg (2005). https://doi.org/10.1007/11513988_48
11. Bytecode Alliance: wasmtime - A Standalone Runtime for WebAssembly (2022). https://github.com/bytecodealliance/wasmtime. Accessed Dec 2022
12. Carbonneaux, Q., Hoffmann, J., Shao, Z.: Compositional certified resource bounds. In: Proceedings of the 36th ACM SIGPLAN Conference on Programming Language Design and Implementation, pp. 467–478. ACM, New York (2015)
13. Cocke, J.: Global common subexpression elimination. In: Proceedings of a Symposium on Compiler Optimization, pp. 20–24. ACM, New York (1970)
14. Cooper, K.D., Torczon, L.: Engineering a Compiler. Elsevier, Burlington (2011)
15. Cullmann, C., Martin, F.: Data-flow based detection of loop bounds. In: 7th International Workshop on Worst-Case Execution Time Analysis (WCET'07). Schloss Dagstuhl-Leibniz-Zentrum für Informatik (2007)
16. Cytron, R., Ferrante, J., Rosen, B.K., Wegman, M.N., Zadeck, F.K.: An efficient method of computing static single assignment form. In: Proceedings of the 16th ACM SIGPLAN-SIGACT Symposium on Principles of Programming Languages, pp. 25–35. ACM, New York (1989)

17. Haas, A., et al.: Bringing the web up to speed with WebAssembly. In: Proceedings of the 38th ACM SIGPLAN Conference on Programming Language Design and Implementation, pp. 185–200. ACM, New York (2017)
18. Hoffmann, J., Aehlig, K., Hofmann, M.: Multivariate amortized resource analysis. In: Proceedings of the 38th Annual ACM SIGPLAN-SIGACT Symposium on Principles of Programming Languages, pp. 357–370. ACM, New York (2011)
19. Hoffmann, J., Das, A., Weng, S.C.: Towards automatic resource bound analysis for OCaml. In: Proceedings of the 44th ACM SIGPLAN Symposium on Principles of Programming Languages, pp. 359–373. ACM, New York (2017)
20. Keith S. Thompson: Dhrystone v2.1 (2022). https://github.com/Keith-S-Thompson/dhrystone/tree/master/v2.1. Accessed Dec 2022
21. Lucas, S.: The origins of the halting problem. J. Logical Algebraic Methods Program. **121**, 100687 (2021)
22. Meyer, F., Hark, M., Giesl, J.: Inferring expected runtimes of probabilistic integer programs using expected sizes. In: TACAS 2021. LNCS, vol. 12651, pp. 250–269. Springer, Cham (2021). https://doi.org/10.1007/978-3-030-72016-2_14
23. musl: musl libc (2023). https://musl.libc.org/. Accessed May 2023
24. Sinn, M., Zuleger, F., Veith, H.: A simple and scalable static analysis for bound analysis and amortized complexity analysis. In: Biere, A., Bloem, R. (eds.) CAV 2014. LNCS, vol. 8559, pp. 745–761. Springer, Cham (2014). https://doi.org/10.1007/978-3-319-08867-9_50
25. WebAssembly Community Group: WebAssembly Introduction (2020). https://webassembly.github.io/spec/core/intro/introduction.html. Accessed Dec 2022
26. Wegbreit, B.: Mechanical program analysis. Commun. ACM **18**(9), 528–539 (1975)
27. Weiser, M.: Program slicing. IEEE Trans. Softw. Eng. **SE-10**(4), 352–357 (1984)

Author Index

C. Pit-Claudel and K. Kosaian (Eds.): VSTTE 2025, LNCS 16499, p. 101, 2026.
https://doi.org/10.1007/978-3-032-27340-6